Smiljan Radić: BESTIARY

First published in Japan on July 7, 2016

Author: Smiljan Radić

Publisher: Toru Kato
TOTO Publishing (TOTO LTD.)
TOTO Nogizaka Bldg., 2F, 1-24-3 Minami-Aoyama
Minato-ku, Tokyo 107-0062, Japan
[Sales] Telephone: +81-3-3402-7138
Facsimile: +81-3-3402-7187
[Editorial] Telephone: +81-3-3497-1010
URL: http://www.toto.co.jp/publishing/
Book Designer: Yoshiaki Irobe, Hiroshi Homma (Nippon Design Center, Inc. Irobe Design Institute)
Printer: Sannichi Printing Co., Ltd.

Except as permitted under copyright law, this book may not be reproduced,
in whole or in part, in any form or by any means, including photocopying, scanning, digitizing,
or otherwise, without prior permission. Scanning or digitizing this book through a third party,
even for personal or home use, is also strictly prohibited.
The list price is indicated on the cover.

ISBN978-4-88706-360-0

Smiljan Radić BESTIARY

スミルハン・ラディック　寓話集

Preface: Bestiary

It seems every good illustration is the image of a momentary conviction. Whatever the technique used -drawings, models, photographs- the effect on the surrounding area is civilising. To illustrate is to civilise, it is to construct the imaginary from a fully unattainable state. A good illustration is always the diffuse multiplication of the memory of an object.

The book entitled Bestiary is a collection of these moments of conviction present in my work. The name refers to medieval bestiaries, which were illustrated books, true compendiums of fantastic beasts drawn from popular imagination and thus impossible to simply "spot" in the real world.

Our Bestiary is a family of models built in wood by the architect Alejandro Lüer based on projects designed in my studio.

Some projects and models of the ones shown here began life as illustrations of texts that I love. They were made as an exercise in interpretation, for no definite reason and without the intention that they should serve some purpose. Coincidence has led to some of them being built years later and some others are on their way to being built.

These models of interpretation, actual uncertain and formal tests, have been the starting point for new projects. Others have formed part of a final presentation shown to clients. The extremes of the process a project follows, the beginning and the end, are treated with the same precision and neatness in these wooden models, simply because we believe that each of them presents an exact conviction about an architecture project.

Smiljan Radić

序文　寓話集

よく描けた挿画には、描き手の脳裏をかすめた確信らしきものが、必ず現れているように思う。どんな方法で描かれていようと──ドローイングであれ、模型であれ、写真であれ──その絵は周囲に啓蒙的な影響を与える。描くことで人を啓蒙し、まったくの無の状態から虚構を構築する。よく描けた挿画には、必ずその対象物の記憶が充満しているものだ。

『寓話集』と題した本書は、私の作品に現れた、こうした確信の瞬間の寄せ集めである。ちなみに本来のBESTIARY（中世の動物寓話集）は、空想上の獣や怪物、つまり現実世界では目にすることのできない生き物を網羅した図鑑のようなものであった。

このたびこの『寓話集』に収められた、私たちの設計したプロジェクトのいくつかを、建築家のアレハンドロ・リューエルが美しい木製模型に仕立ててくれた。

ここに収められたプロジェクトや模型の中には、私の気に入りの文章の挿画から生まれたものもある。これらはあくまで解釈の一環として制作した模型なので、その背景にはこれといった根拠もなければ、用途も想定されていない。数年後に実現に至った、あるいは実現に向けて動き出したプロジェクトもあるが、それは単に巡り合わせがよかっただけのことだ。

模型は単に、ひとつの解釈、検討中の未定の形態にすぎない。中にはプロジェクトの出発点となった模型もあれば、施主への最終プレゼンテーションに用いられた模型もある。プロジェクトを進める間は首尾一貫して、これらの木製模型並みの精度と整然さを心掛けた。つまり私たちにとってはどの模型も、まさしくその建築プロジェクトに対する確信の現れなのである。

スミルハン・ラディック

Preface: Bestiary ———————————————————— 4

Tent

#01   NAVE, Performing Arts Hall ———————————— 10

#02   Room ——————————————————————— 34

#03   Bío Bío Regional Theatre ——————————————— 52

Membrane Roof

#04   Chilean Museum of Pre-Columbia Art Extensions —————— 72

#05   Meeting Point ————————————————————— 94

#06   Environmental Science Museum Guadalajara Project ———— 104

Refuge

#07   House for the Poem of the Right Angle ———————— 118

#08   The Boy Hidden in a Fish ————————————— 140

#09   The Boy Hidden in an Egg ————————————— 150

#10   The Selfish Giant's Castle ————————————— 154

#11   Serpentine Gallery Pavilion 2014 ————————— 160

Tower

#12   Santiago Antenna Tower Project ————————— 186

#13   Fragile ————————————————————— 200

#14   Tower Light Bulbs ————————————————— 206

Stone

#15   Mestizo Restaurant ———————————————— 214

#16   Red Stone House ————————————————— 238

Recent Works

#17   House of Wood ————————————————— 258

#18   Russo Park Project ———————————————— 284

Correspondence with Sou Fujimoto ————————— 298

Project Data ———————————————————— 308

Credit ——————————————————————— 310

Profile ——————————————————————— 311

序文 寓話集 ———————————————————————————————— 4

テント

#01　NAVE——パフォーミング・アーツ・ホール ———————————— 10

#02　ルーム ——————————————————————————————— 34

#03　ビオビオ市民劇場 ———————————————————————— 52

膜屋根

#04　チリ・プレコロンビア芸術博物館の拡張 ———————————— 72

#05　ミーティング・ポイント ———————————————————— 94

#06　グアダラハラ環境科学博物館計画案 ——————————————— 104

隠れ家

#07　直角の詩に捧ぐ家 ———————————————————————— 118

#08　魚に隠れた少年 ————————————————————————— 140

#09　卵に隠れた少年 ————————————————————————— 150

#10　わがままな大男の城 —————————————————————— 154

#11　サーペンタイン・ギャラリー・パヴィリオン2014 ——————— 160

タワー

#12　サンティアゴ・アンテナ・タワー計画案 ————————————— 186

#13　フラジャイル ————————————————————————— 200

#14　ランプの塔 —————————————————————————— 206

石

#15　メスチーソ・レストラン ———————————————————— 214

#16　レッド・ストーン・ハウス ——————————————————— 238

近作

#17　木の家 ———————————————————————————— 258

#18　ルッソ・パーク・プロジェクト ————————————————— 284

藤本壮介との往復書簡 ——————————————————————— 298

作品データ ———————————————————————————— 308

クレジット ———————————————————————————— 310

略歴 —————————————————————————————— 311

Tent
テント

#01

NAVE, Performing Arts Hall

2015
Santiago, Chile

The project for this experimental arts hall proposes an emptying operation, in which the same municipal regulations that halted the building's renovation and brought on its current disrepair are used to our advantage. The facade is the only structure that remained partially intact after the fire in 2006 and the earthquake in 2010. These disasters opened up the interior and erased forever the remains of eight houses that had occupied the site.

The project totally empties the property, reproducing the original facade until it is complete in every detail, making it a sort of friendly disguise. The city can be seen from inside through the gaps, forming part of the backdrop for some of the events. Few structural elements touch the ground on the first floor: the lift, a staircase and the support wall for mobile tiers. The pathway for the theatrical audience hangs from a center girder and culminates on the roof-terrace, proposed for a popular circus. Everything seems to have been measured from above.
The circus is the first, the most primitive and the most austere place imaginable for shows. A strange *objet trouvé*, a long way from its home, will appear above the theatre, a source of delight for the neighborhood. The rehearsal rooms, offices and services occupy other houses in the complex, turning the entire building as it stands into a new internally interrelated organism.

NAVE ── パフォーミング・アーツ・ホール
2015
チリ、サンティアゴ

この実験的なホールのプロジェクトでは、建物をいったん空(から)にする。かつてこの建物の改修を阻み、結果的にそれを劣化に導いた市の条例（歴史的建造物保護指定）を、こうして逆手に取ることにした。2006年の火事に続いて2010年には地震に見舞われてもなお、ほぼ無傷といえる構造体はファサードのみである。相次ぐ災害によって建物内部は吹きさらしになり、そこにあった8戸（全体の4分の1）の住宅は跡形もなく消えた。

このプロジェクトでは建物を完全に空にし、オリジナルのファサードを細大漏らさず忠実に復元することで、親しみやすい装いに仕立てる。建物内部から隙間越しに見える町並みは、イベント時には背景の一部になる。1階ではいくつかの構造的要素（エレベーター、階段、スタンド席を支える壁）が、じかに地面に接している。中央の大梁に吊るされた観客用の通路は、屋上のサーカス会場へ至る。この屋上を基準に全体が計画されていったようなものだ。サーカステントは、考えられる限り最古の素朴な興行場である。この屋上に辿り着いた奇妙なファウンド・オブジェクトは、近隣住民に尽きせぬ喜びを与えるだろう。リハーサル室、オフィス、設備はそれぞれ施設内の既存の住宅跡に配置され、こうして建物内部は相互に関係付けられ、建物自体がひとつの有機体に生まれ変わる。

CEDAR WOOD MODEL by ALEJANDRO LÜER

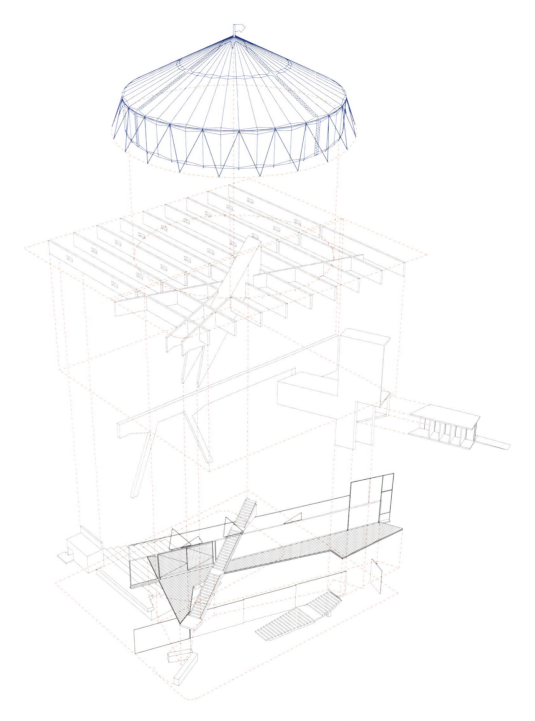

Exploded Isometric

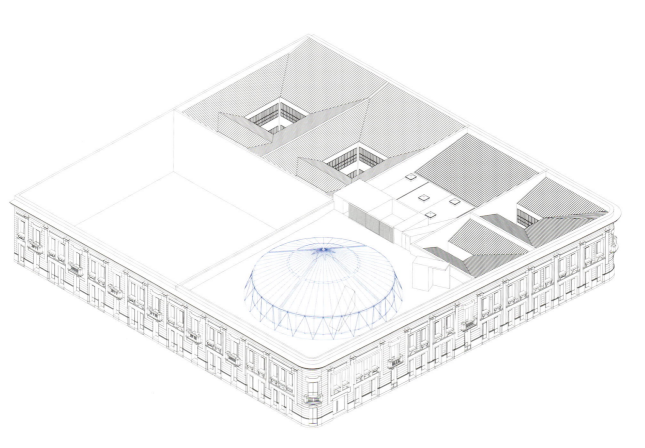

Isometric

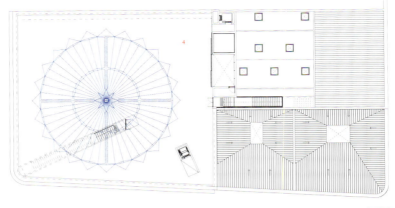

L +10,14

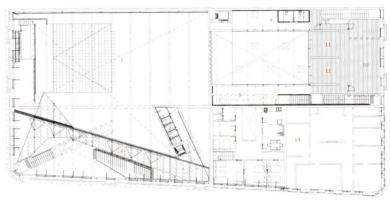

L +3,75

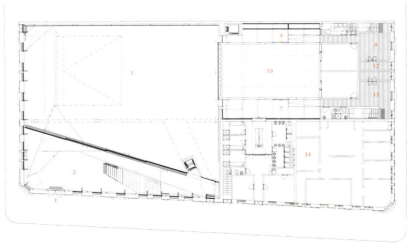

1. Principal Access
2. Lobby
3. Performing Arts Hall
4. Circus Tent
5. Retractil Grandstand
6. Access Bridge
7. Dressing Room
8. Videoteca
9. Kitchen
10. Rehearsal Room
11. Multitask Room
12. Warehouse
13. Office
14. Existing Housing

L +0,00

0 1 2 3 4 5m

N

Plans

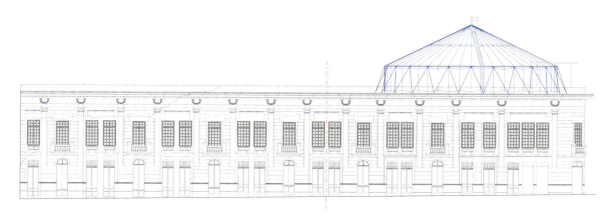

South Elevation

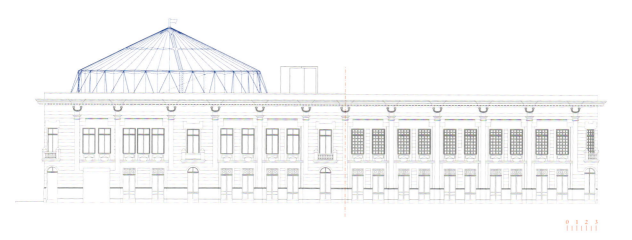

East Elevation

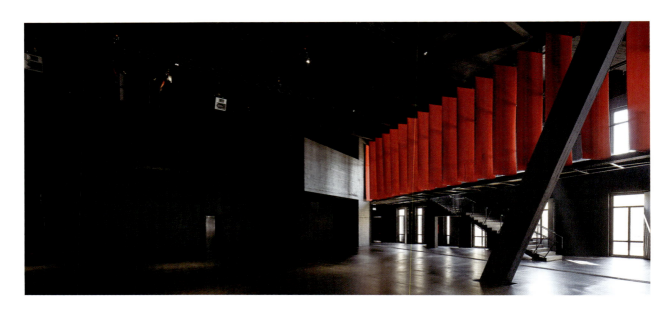

#02

Room

2007
Chiloé Island, Chile

"Eliminating distance kills"——Rene Char

When an inhabitant of Chiloé Island wanted to move house, he used oxen to drag it into the sea. He then used boats to float it to the shore of another island, where he installed it on a previously chosen site, set on boulders. These homes obviously are not related to a specific place, a view or a landscape, but to the recognition of a whole territory in which they can easily move or float, if you will. Architecture often does not need a place: it needs a territory that can be either physical or intellectual.

    The *Room* is a refuge, and like all refuges, it attempts to maintain a distance. The Mount Athos monasteries, the monks' caves in Meteora, a bullock driver's shelter in the Andes or perhaps Toyo Ito's pao for the Nomad Women in Tokyo are all examples of this attempt.

    The *Room* was moved piece by piece by boat, oxen and by hand, carried manually over a two month period to a site far from any trace of civilization, in the middle of the only clearing in the elm forest on the site. Its Bookcase Structure, built nail-less with timber planks, presumably like the old folk style, carries the weight of everything that the *Room* should hold, not only the result of the building itself, but also the vestiges and memories built up on its walls by use. The *Room* does not favour any view in particular, because there is nothing to see around it, just the uniform green foliage in the spot where the building seems to have run aground.

    Ten years later, we enlarged the second floor of the *Room* with a red marquee to transform it into a roost. This extension related its image to the cottages we found scattered among the forests on Chiloé Island: simple volumes in rain-washed timber, with tin sheet gabled roofs that are sometimes painted red.

Granary Building in Chiloé Island

ルーム
2007
チリ、チロエ島

「隔たりを取り去ることは殺すこと」── ルネ・シャール

チロエ島に暮らすひとりの男が家を移築しようとして、海辺までこれを雄牛に引かせた。そこからはボートに積んで別の島の岸辺まで運び、前から目を付けていた敷地に巨石を敷き、その上に家を設置した。この手の住居は言うまでもなく、特定の場所とも眺めとも風景とも無縁だが、例えばその領域内なら家を容易に動かしたり場合によっては浮かべたりできると考える人間の空間認識とは結び付いている。建築には場所が必要とは限らない。必要なのは、人間が身体か頭のどちらかで認識することのできる領域である。

　この「ルーム」は隠れ家であり、そして世の隠れ家の例にもれず、外界と一定の距離を保とうとする。そうした意図で建てられたものには、例えばギリシャのアトス山の修道院、修道士が隠遁するメテオラの洞窟、アンデス山脈の牛追いが暮らす小屋、そしてたぶん伊東豊雄の「東京遊牧少女の包（パオ）」などがある。

　この「ルーム」の移築のために、ふた月がかりでボートと雄牛を何往復もさせながら手作業で建材を運んだ。移築先は文明の手が一切及んでいない、楡の森に唯一ぽかりと残されていた空地である。釘を一切打たずに厚板を組み上げた書架構造は、昔の民俗様式のようなもので、「ルーム」がこの先抱えるであろう重みをすべてこの構造が受け止めることになる。建物の自重のみならず、住まわれるうちにその壁に積み上がっていくことになる諸々の痕跡や記憶の重みを、である。「ルーム」からの眺めに優先順位は付けられていない。なぜなら周りにはとりたてて見るべきものがなく、緑の葉が一面に茂っているだけだから。むしろ建物がその緑の海に座礁してしまったようにも見える。

　10年が経ち、この「ルーム」に2階を増築することになったので、赤いテントを張って鶏舎風にした。この増築部分は、イメージとしてはチロエ島の森の中に点在している小屋とも重なる。それらは雨食した木材で出来た単純なヴォリュームにトタンの切妻屋根を載せたもので、その屋根がたまに赤く塗られていたりする。

MINGA - TRADITIONAL HOUSE TRANSPORTATION in CHILOÉ ISLAND

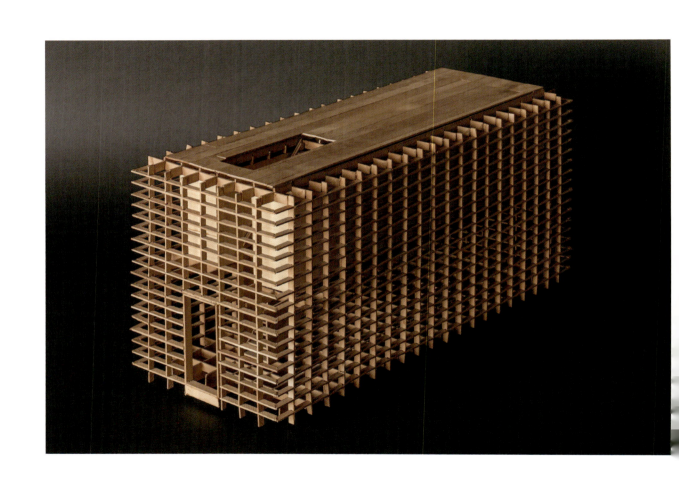

FIRST PROJECT MODEL by SMILJAN RADIĆ

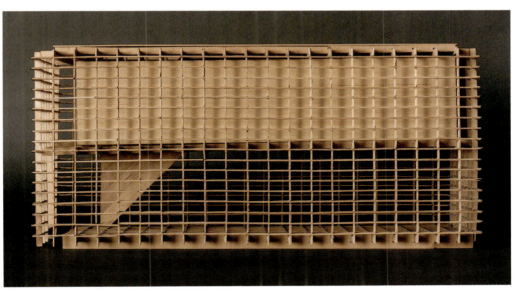

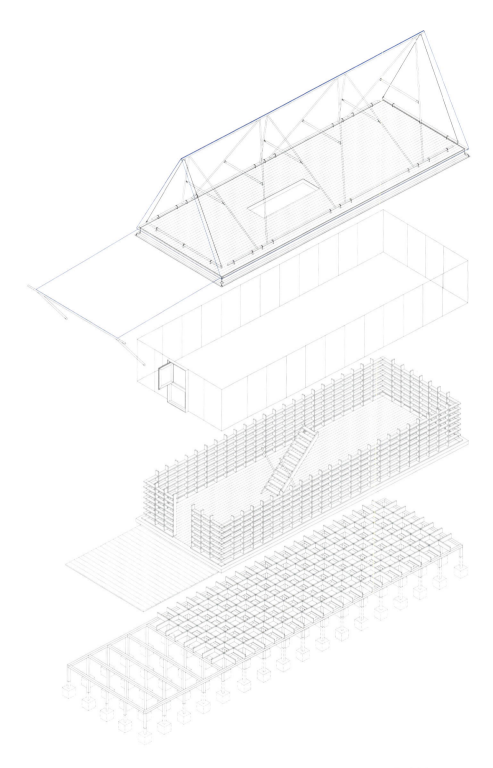

Exploded Isometric

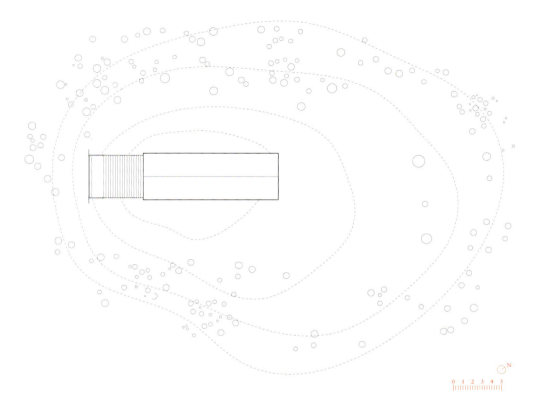

Site Plan

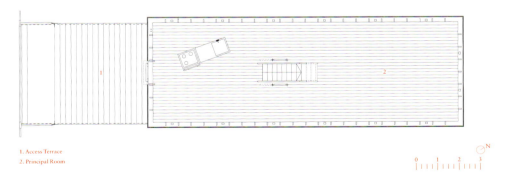

1. Access Terrace
2. Principal Room

Plan Level 1

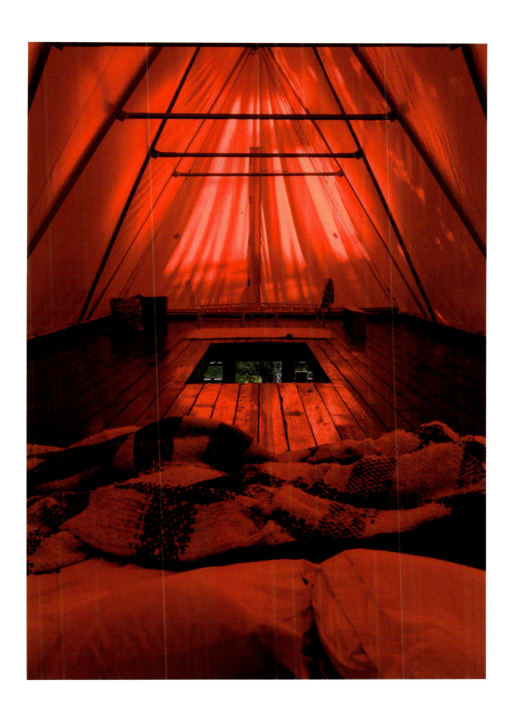

#03

Bío Bío Regional Theatre

2011–
Concepción, Chile

*"Emballage was an attempt to 'sniff out' the nature of the object.
Hiding it, wrapping it."*——Tadeusz Kantor

Our project for the *Bío-Bío Regional Theatre* is the potential skeleton of a wrapped theatre. Inside, the spectator will move/climb on a spatial grid that seems to madly measure/occupy each corner. The theatres themselves are where the sense of saturation diminishes, and the necessary air required for the play returns. A black air, a penumbra with fuzzy boundaries. All this *paraphernalia* surrounding the theatres —regarded as open fields amidst this 3.9x3.9x3.9 m structural grid— is simply a scaffold, like the rear of a stage: the insignificant prop that is usually unseen, hidden. Spectators thus need not to wait to cross the foyer and enter the dark auditorium to open the theatre. The mystery begins before they enter. *Passersby-spectators* only need to see the draped mantle veiling the building to imagine or 'sniff out', as Kantor might put it, that something is hidden inside, or at least believe for a moment that someone walking around inside is accompanied by an experimental process. On the other hand, the actors have access to a flexible type of air. The rooms are given contemporary dimensions, with a few basic mechanical devices to resolve the optimal technical qualities required by the building, which also increase its versatility.

©Tadeusz Kantor

ビオビオ市民劇場
2011-
チリ、コンセプシオン

「梱包(アンバラージュ)は、物体(オブジェ)の本質を〈嗅ぎ当てる〉試みだった。
物体を隠し、包むことで。」──タデウシュ・カントル

「ビオビオ市民劇場」のプロジェクトは、梱包された劇場のスケルトン化を図ったものである。内部では、観客がグリッド状の空間を移動、上昇する。このグリッドが、建物の隅から隅までをきっちり等間隔に区切り、くまなく埋め尽くす。ホールに入った途端にグリッドの飽和感が薄れ、舞台上演に必要な空気が戻ってくる。黒い空気が、事物の輪郭をぼかす薄暗がりが。個々のホール──3.9×3.9×3.9mの構造グリッドに囲われたオープンフィールド──を取り囲むこうした道具立ては、単なる足場組みというか舞台裏のようなものであり、ふつうなら人目に触れない場所に隠されてしまうほどの瑣末な小道具にすぎない。これなら観客は、幕が開くまでの間、ホワイエで待たされずに暗いホールへ入場することができる。この劇場の謎は、まだ建物へ入らぬ内から始まる。道行く観客は、建物に掛けられた覆いを見ただけでその背後に隠されたものを想像し、もしくはカントルの言うように〈嗅ぎ当てる〉か、でなければその内部を歩き回るだけでも良い体験になりそうだとの期待くらいは抱くだろう。一方で役者たちの出入りする空間は、フレキシブルにしてある。諸室は今日的な広さで、必要最小限の機械装置を備えている。この装置によって、建物の技術的な性能が最適化され、ひいては建物の汎用性も向上する。

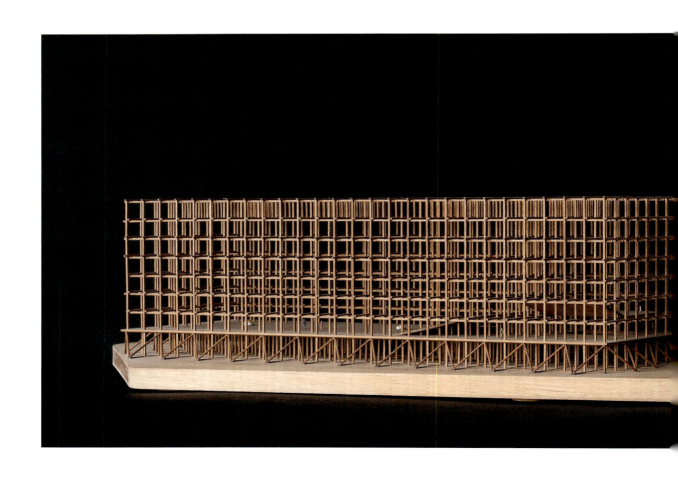

PRELIMINARY CEDAR WOOD MODEL by ALEJANDRO LÜER

FINAL CEDAR WOOD MODEL by ALEJANDRO LÜER

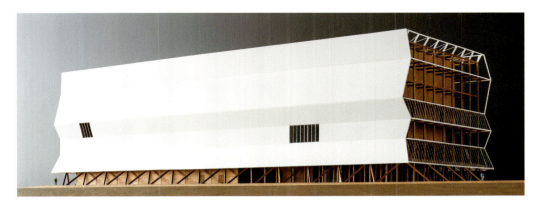

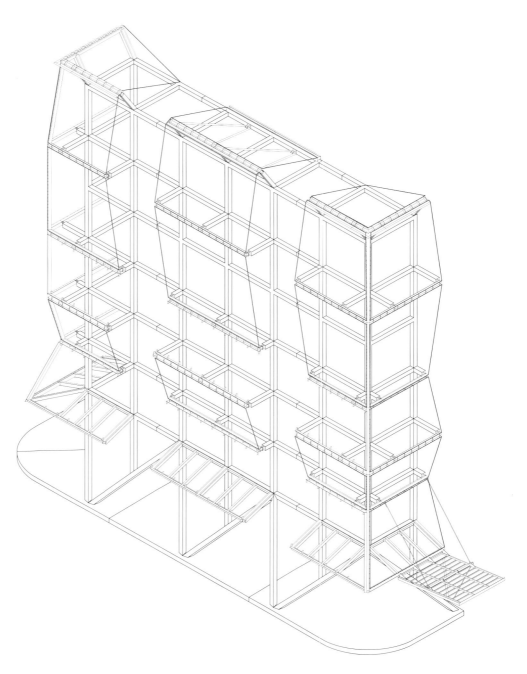

Corner Axonometric, Membrane Detail

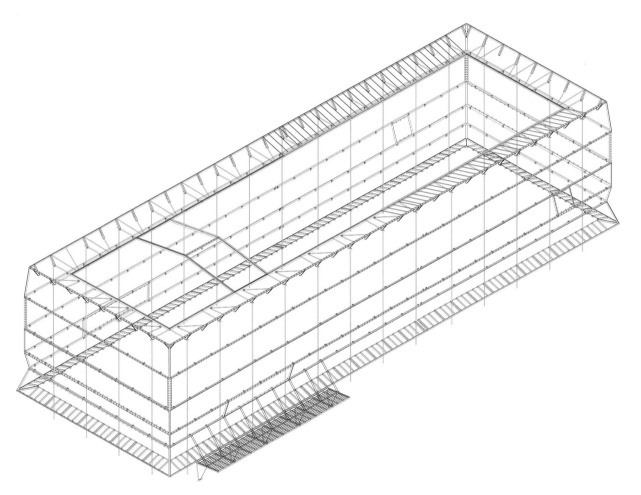

Steel Flame Axonometric

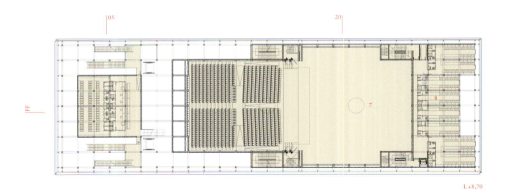

L.+8,70

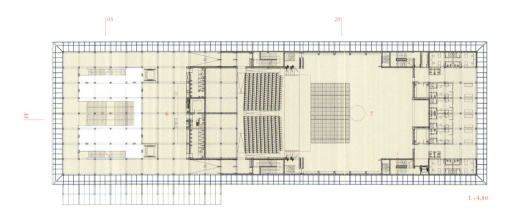

L.+4,80

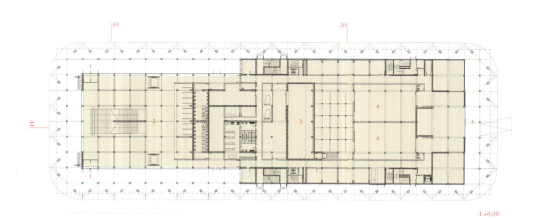

L.+0,00

1. Public Access
2. Access Hall
3. Orchestra Pit
4. Workshop
5. Trucking Access
6. Cafe Teria
7. Main Hall
8. Dressing Room
9. Sub Hall
10. Office
11. Rehearsal Room

Plans

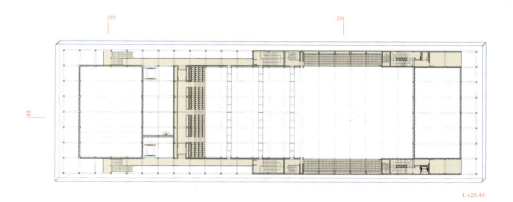

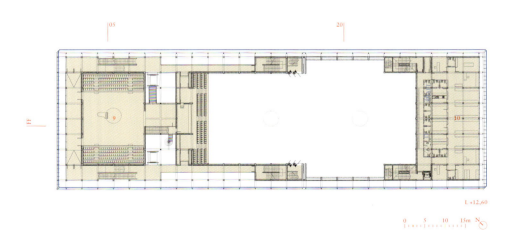

Plans

61

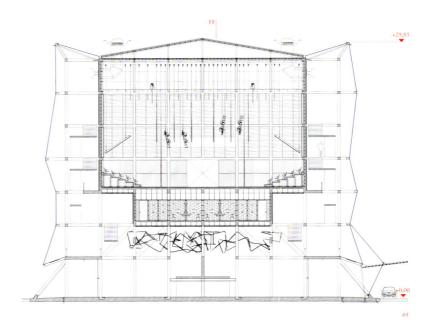

Public Hall Section

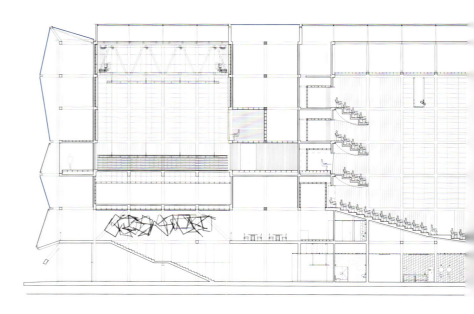

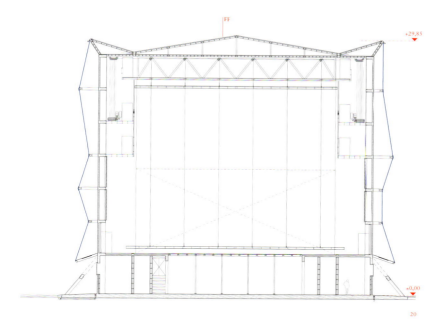

Main Hall Section

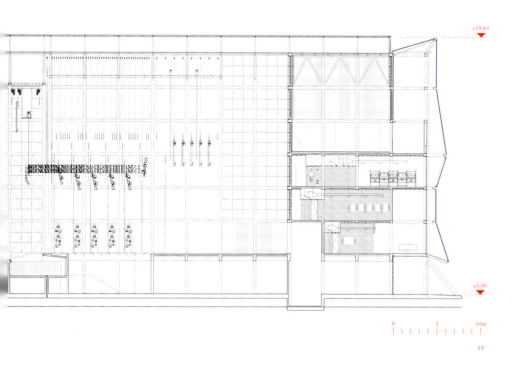

Longuitudinal Section

VIEW of CONSTRUCTION

MODULE 1:1

Membrane Roof
膜屋根

#04

Chilean Museum of Pre-Columbian Art Extensions

2014
Santiago, Chile

The new 'Chile before Chile' room is a unique opportunity to consolidate the institutional building and rework the spatial imaginaries of the Chilean Museum of Pre-Columbian Art, neatly characterizing each of its various areas, one by one. The existing building is organized around two courtyards and an outdoor public gallery on the first floor. Approximately 1000 m² will be added to its exhibition space, along with two underground storage levels beneath the north and south courtyards. The project maintains the current entrance through the public gallery and the north courtyard, which is furnished for the reception, café and shop services, currently confined to the central foyer. In order to include the north courtyard in the usable floor space, it will be roofed with an inflated translucent Low-E ETFE membrane bubble.

 The southern courtyard, on the other hand, will remain an outdoor space, free of restrictive uses. Its floor consists of 2" diameter pebbles set in sand, like the material found in recent archaeological excavations on the site. The entrance hall between the courtyards is freed in order to hold the vertical circulations that lead to each of the museum's four levels. The largest exhibition hall, measuring 38x11x7m., and the storage rooms beneath it are located underground, traversing the length of the building in a unique itinerary called 'Chile before Chile'. Its large size, or rather its lack of definition, will give the museum's exhibition rooms a new scale. A natural penumbra will prevail here, nuanced by light entering through two skylights at each end. It will be built in concrete, stained charcoal grey, and dark IPE wood. Its edges will be blurred on account of the shadows, accentuating its excavated or subterranean condition. In contrast to this underground situation, the pre-existing above-ground rooms will receive natural lighting through windows facing the street and the courtyards, which were previously blocked completely or partially.

チリ・プレコロンビア芸術博物館の拡張

2014
チリ、サンティアゴ

〈チリ以前のチリ（スペイン植民地以前のチリ）〉展示室の新設を契機に、既存の公共施設を整理統合し、なおかつチリ・プレコロンビア芸術博物館の内部空間を改修し、エリアごとに特徴をもたせることになった。既存建物の平面は、1階にあるふたつの中庭のギャラリーを取り囲むように構成されている。今回はそこにおよそ1,000㎡の展示スペースを追加すると同時に、南北それぞれの中庭の真下に地下収蔵庫を増設する。現行の入館経路はパブリックなアーケードを抜けて北側の中庭へ至っているが、これはそのまま残し、ただし北側の中庭には造作を施し、現在中央ホワイエに詰め込まれたレセプション、カフェ、ショップをそこへ移設する。この北側の中庭を有効床面積として取り込むべく、屋根を架け、半透明のLow-E低放射率フッ素樹脂（テフロン）膜を張る。

一方、南側の中庭は屋外空間のままにし、用途も限定しない。足元には、考古学調査で発掘されたばかりのような直径5cmの玉石を砂地の上に敷き詰める。両中庭に挟まれたエントランスホールを開放し、そこに全4階にまたがる垂直動線を通す。広さ38×11×7mの大展示室とその真下に併設される収蔵庫をそっくり地下に収め、建物の長手方向に配置する。これが同博物館ならではの、いわゆる〈チリ以前のチリ〉を訪ねる経路となる。この展示室の規模の大きさというか茫漠としたところが、ほかの展示室にはない新鮮なスケールをもたらす。展示室は自然な薄暗がりに包まれているが、両端にある各トップライトから射す光がそこにニュアンスを添える。躯体のコンクリートをチャコールグレーで着色し、さらに濃色の木材を張る。壁の輪郭は影になってぼかされるので、いかにも地中めいた雰囲気になる。この地下部分に対して地上にある既存の諸室には、窓越しに採光する。街路や中庭に面したこれらの窓は、以前は部分的に、もしくは完全に塞がれていた。

PRELIMINARY CEDAR WOOD MODEL by ALEJANDRO LÜER

1. Armas Plaza (Main Square Of Santiago)
2. Metropolitan Cathedral
3. Ex-Congressional District Of Chile
4. Tribunes Of Justice
5. Chilean Museum Of Pre-Columbian Art
6. City Hall Of Santiago
7. National Historical Museum

Site Plan

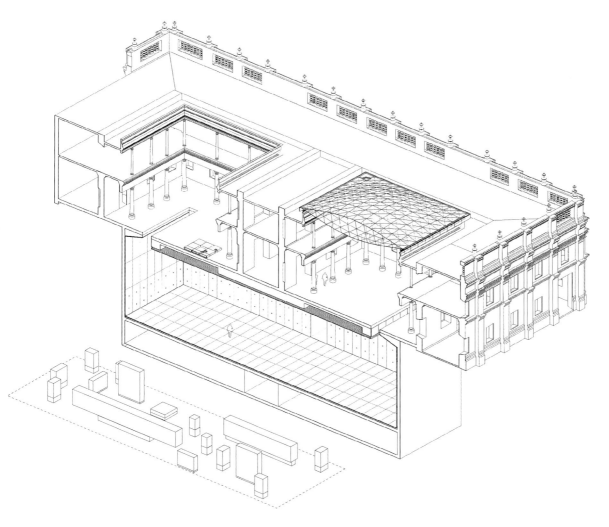

Exploded Isometric

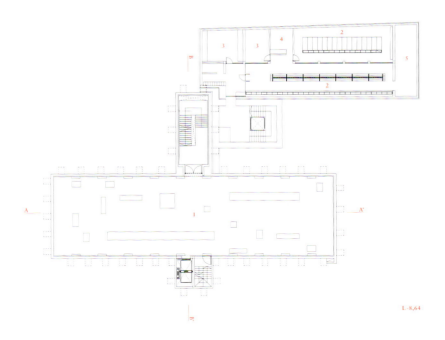

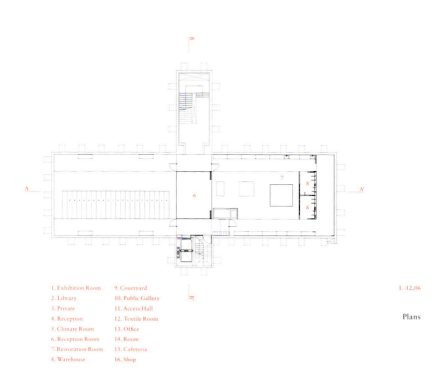

1. Exhibition Room
2. Library
3. Private
4. Reception
5. Climate Room
6. Reception Room
7. Restoration Room
8. Warehouse
9. Courtyard
10. Public Gallery
11. Access Hall
12. Textile Room
13. Office
14. Room
15. Cafeteria
16. Shop

Plans

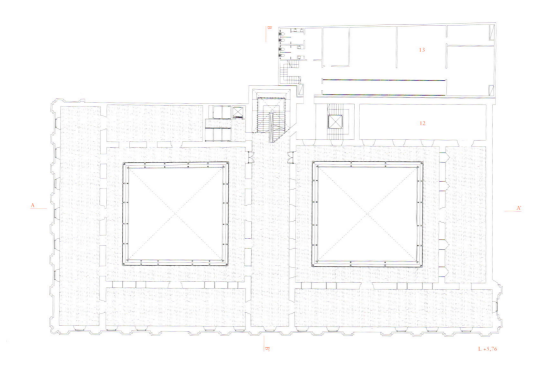

Plans

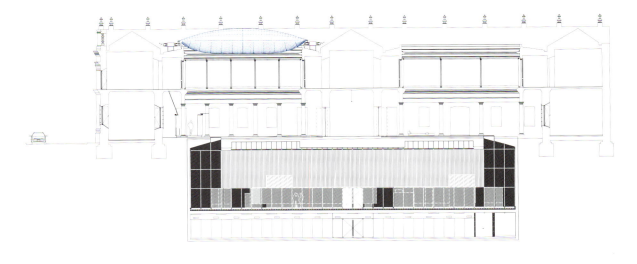

Longitudinal Section A

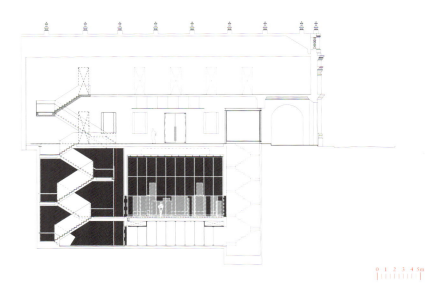

Cross Sectiones B

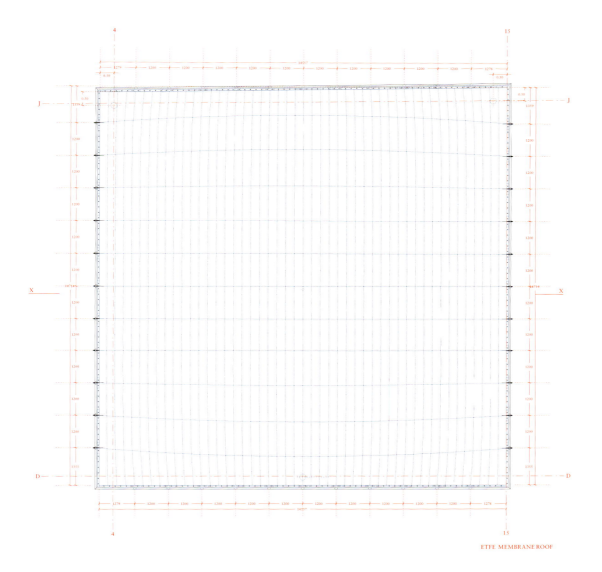

ETFE MEMBRANE ROOF

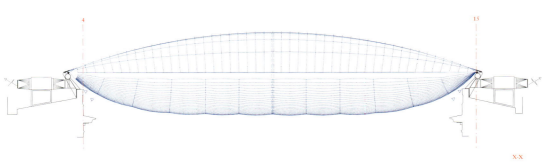

X-X

Membrane Roof Detail

#05

Meeting Point
2009

The last great earthquake in Chile occurred on November 14, 2007 at 12:40 pm, with an intensity of 7.7 degrees on the Richter scale. Its epicenter was in the Atacama Desert town of Quillagua, and it covered 1200 km. A reasonable period of time has passed since that emergency, but crowded, originally interim camps can still be found in the landscape. Sad but fast and effective camps built for the purpose by the Armed Forces. These camps have been the basis and the direct physical point of reference for the reconstruction of the small villages affected by the earthquake. The victims thus begin rebuilding their villages with a distrust in their past —literally scattered across the land—, distrust in their poor building techniques linked to adobe and stone, overshadowed by the new logic of low cost organization. However, in these villages, traditional techniques happen to be the most appropriate and perhaps the only ones capable of permitting community involvement in the creative work of recovery from emergencies. Still in the shadow of the 2010 earthquake, perhaps we should now realize that the role of the designer is to spend time permanently studying solutions for these disasters, not only under the macabre incentive of the immediate event. This study may involve collaborating with the slow but definitive reconstruction work of towns using appropriate techniques. We can also try to solve immediate problems, providing not only low-cost individual or family shelters but also spontaneous emergency townships which facilitate the reunion and projects signs of protection for the community: precincts that can be identified as public property. Our Meeting Point project, created for the 'Crossing Dialogues for Emergency Architecture' exhibition at the National Art Museum of China in Beijing, aims to create *spontaneous institutions*. Its formal value is nothing more than the ugly, traditional bandstands that decorate every self-respecting town square in Chile. They are used by local orchestras at weekends, for political speeches, played chess and telling jokes.

ミーティング・ポイント

2009

チリで最後に巨大地震が起きたのは2007年11月14日午後12時40分、地震の規模はマグニ
チュード7.7だった。震源地はアタカマ砂漠のキジャグア村で、震源域は1,200kmに達した。
危機的状態からいろいろあったにせよ、一定の時間が経った今もなお一帯には仮設集落が点
在する。わびしい集落だが、国防軍はこれをその目的どおりに迅速かつ大量に建設したので
あった。被災地の小さな村々は、こうした仮設集落の建物をそれこそ参考にして村の再建に
乗り出した。そしていざ工事を始めると、被災者たちは――文字どおり大地の上に散乱した
――過去への不信感、ローコストな工法が現れたせいで見劣りしてしまった日干しれんがと
石を用いた古拙な工法への不信感を募らせていく。けれどもこの村々に最も適しているのは
むしろ在来工法であり、それに多分ほかの工法ではコミュニティ参加による自力再建は果た
せそうにない。2010年に再び地震に見舞われた今、私たちデザイナーもそろそろ災害時の
対処法を土壇場になってからではなく常日頃から検討しておくことを職務として自覚すべき
なのだろう。例えば、町の復興を徐々にではあるが着実に進めるためには、どんな技術を用
いることが適切かといったことを事前に調べるなどして。もちろん緊急問題に取り組むこと
もあるだろう。その場合、個人ないし家族向けの廉価なシェルターをつくる以外にも、例え
ば被災者が避難居住区を自発的につくる作業を手助けして、そこを人びとの再会の場に、コ
ミュニティがまるごと避難できるような公有地的な領域にすることもできる。北京の中国美
術館で開かれた「Crossing Dialogues for Emergency Architecture（国際応急建築設計）」展
への出展作「ミーティング・ポイント」では、自力建設型の公共施設をつくることにした。形
態としては、昔ながらの不格好な野外ステージにすぎない。チリ各地の町では、こうした野
外ステージが誇らしげに広場を飾っている。週末になると、ステージ上では地元の楽団が演
奏し、政治演説が行われ、チェス競技が開かれ、お笑い芸が披露される。

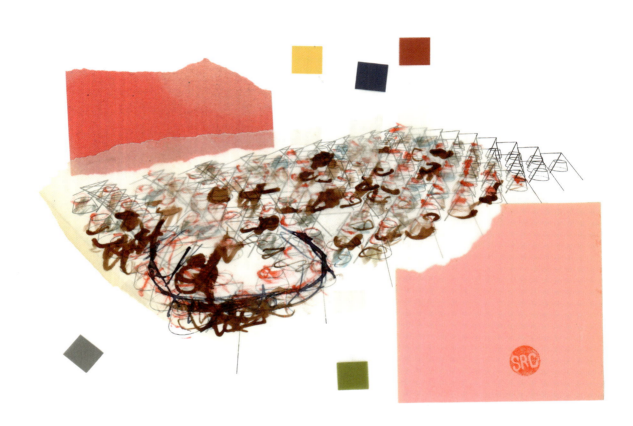

MASTER VIEW of EMERGENCY CITY

MASTER VIEW of EMERGENCY CITY

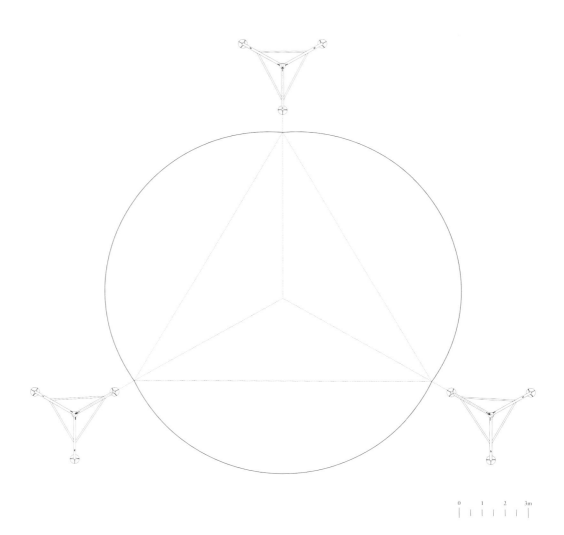

Meeting Point Plan

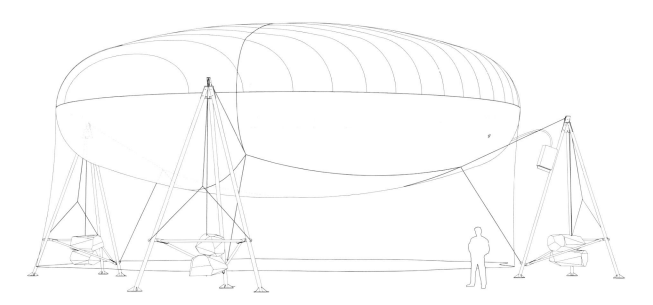

Meeting Point View

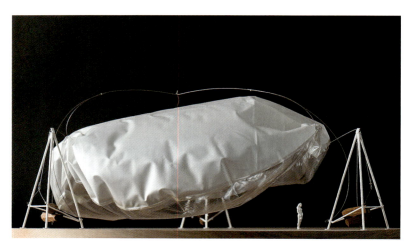

FINAL MODEL by ALEJANDRO LÜER

#06

Environmental Science Museum Guadalajara Project

2011
Jalisco, México

Several natural systems converge in Jalisco state, near the narrowest point of the American continent. Our project was presented as a container in which these confluences and their relations with the urban system would be represented to encourage the community to foster bonds of care and coexistence. We suggested that the learning and interpretation process in the Museum should be treated as a system of signs and stimuli along a wandering route, encouraging visitors to use their innate resources for comprehension to generate a story of their own that would facilitate different pathwaysof intellectual entry to the exhibition. We avoided the conventional configuration of public display precincts —airtight, hierarchical and connected linearly through doorways—. Instead, we proposed a spatial simultaneity at every level to increase the complexity of the potential relationships. The building was to be the 'map of a new world' that would be learned and interpreted during every visit. First, as a communal experience 'under one sky' —materialized by the building's single roof and a system of large inflated ETFE membrane tubes—, and secondly, as an individual wandering experience 'on new ground'— consisting of a continuous, arbitrary topography, which would draw its geometric pattern from the amazing *Ines Table* designed by Enric Miralles, as we did later on in the *SheHouse* project.

グアダラハラ環境科学博物館計画案

2011
メキシコ、ハリスコ

アメリカ大陸がすぼまる寸前の位置にあるハリスコ州には、複数の自然生態系が集まっている。このプロジェクトはそうした生態系を都市システムと併置して見せるための器であり、つまりこの展示によって地域社会には自然との絆を育み、共存することを学んでもらう。見学者が展示内容を少しずつ学習・理解できるようにサイン計画を立て、経路を蛇行させて退屈させないようにしてあるので、これにより見学者はもち前の読解力に従って自分なりの物語を紡ぎながら、めいめいの知的興味に従って展示と向き合うことになる。ここでは展示エリアを型どおりの──閉鎖的な空間をそれぞれの出入り口部分で串刺しにして階層的に並べた──配置にはしていない。代わりに、どの階でも空間を同期させ、それらが複雑に絡み合うようにした。ここでは建物そのものを〈新世界の地図〉に仕立て、訪れるたびに新しい発見や解釈が生ずるようにしている。まずは〈ひとつ空の下〉──建物を覆う1枚の大屋根の下にチューブ状のフッ素樹脂（テフロン）膜を並べたもの──で体験を共有し、次に〈新しい大地の上〉を思い思いに歩き回ることで。こちらのひと続きの大地については、後に「SheHouse」でもそうしたように、エンリック・ミラージェスのデザインした傑作「Ines Table」の平面形状を下敷きにした。

CONTEXT MODEL by ALEJANDRO LÜER

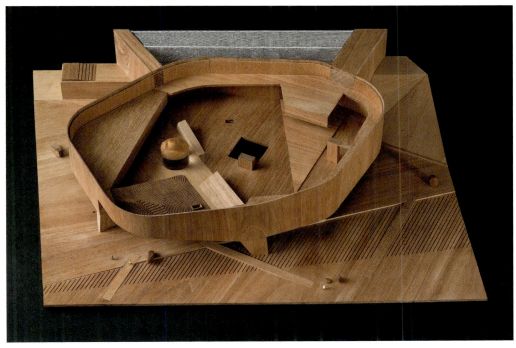

PRELIMINARY SKETCH

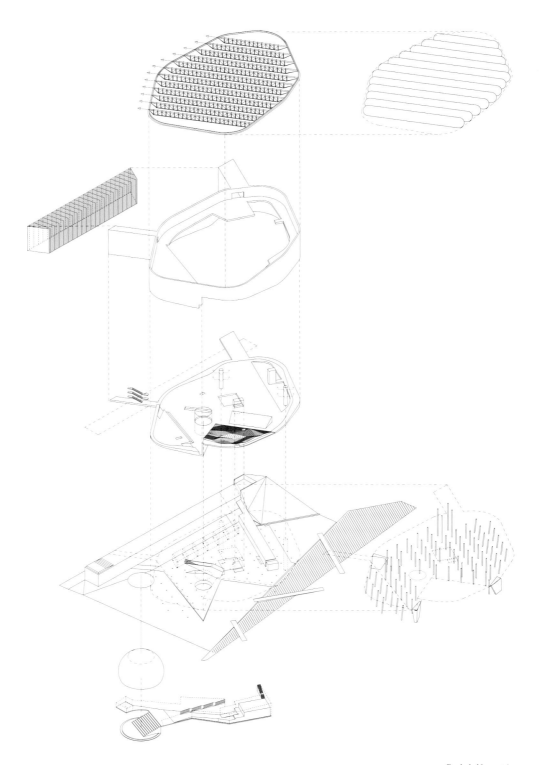

Exploded Isometric

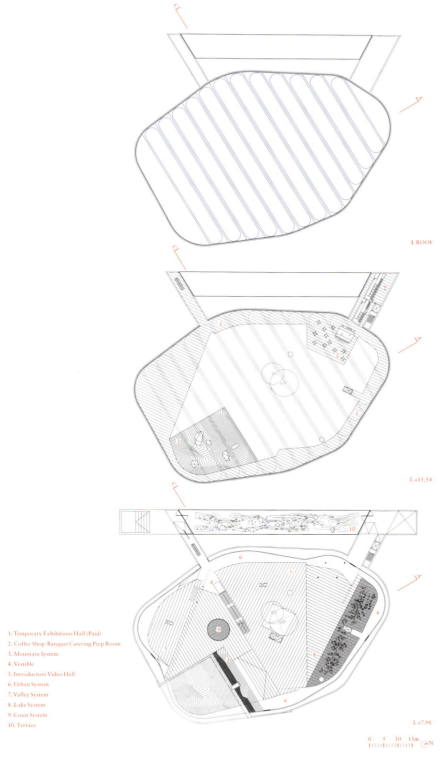

Plans

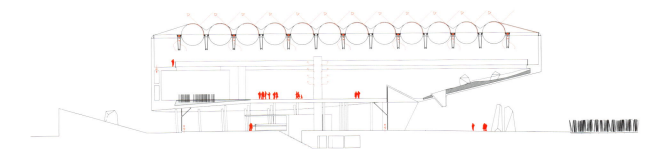

Longitudinal Section A

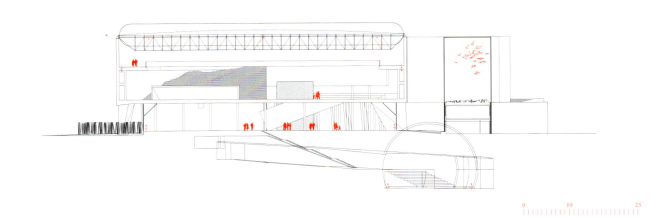

Cross Section C

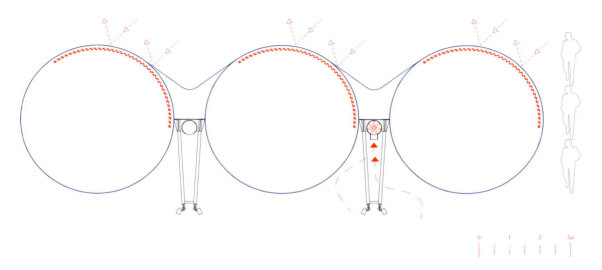

Pneuma Ticary Pre-Stressed Roof Structure Detail

Refuge
隠れ家

#07

House for the Poem of the Right Angle

2012
Vilches, Chile

The *House for the Poem of the Right Angle* is the last refuge we have designed; it is a blind case facing a privileged landscape of mountains and oak woods. The house assumes that the inhabitant knows where the river flows, but does not see it because he simply knows about it, it is permanently recognized at a distance.

The *House for the Poem of the Right Angle* refers to the lithograph illustrating the chapter entitled Flesh of the poem by Le Corbusier. This image of earth colors formally shows a sort of cave. An elementary shelter roofed by the hand-vault of a man laying on its back, the floor is his body and on the background a nude woman looks the landscape traversed by a cloud which opens the darkness of the indoor environment. The opacity of this interior, the wild suggested materiality and mostly calm in its atmosphere were a guide to design the House for the Poem of the Right Angle.

Poem of the Right Angle-chapter c2, Le Corbusier

直角の詩に捧ぐ家

2012
チリ、ビルチェス

「直角の詩に捧ぐ家」は、私たちがデザインした最新の隠れ家である。それは山々の絶景とオーク林を望む、閉じた箱である。住まい手には、いつなん時も川がどこを流れているかが、たとえ離れた所に居ても分かっている。そうした前提でこの家はつくられている。

　「直角の詩に捧ぐ家」の参考にしたのが、ル・コルビュジエの詩画集の「肉体」と題した章に添えられたリトグラフである。アースカラーで描かれたこの絵には、洞窟らしきものが描かれている。原始的なシェルターを覆うように、仰向けになった男が手をかざしている。床らしきものは実は男の胴体で、奥に居る裸婦が振り向く視線の先にはたなびく雲があり、そしてこの雲が暗い洞窟内部に光を灯している。光の射さない内部、粗野な物質性、おおむね平穏な雰囲気。この3つを手掛かりにして「直角の詩に捧ぐ家」をデザインした。

FINAL CEDAR WOOD MODEL by ALEJANDRO LÜER

PROJECT SKETCH

PROJECT SKETCH

BUILDING CONSTRUCTION STAGE

Exploded Facade

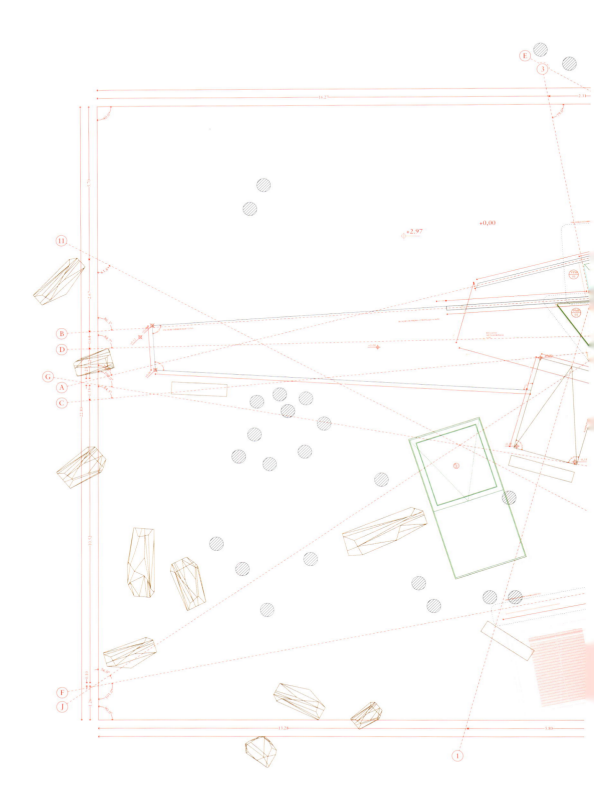

Floor Plan

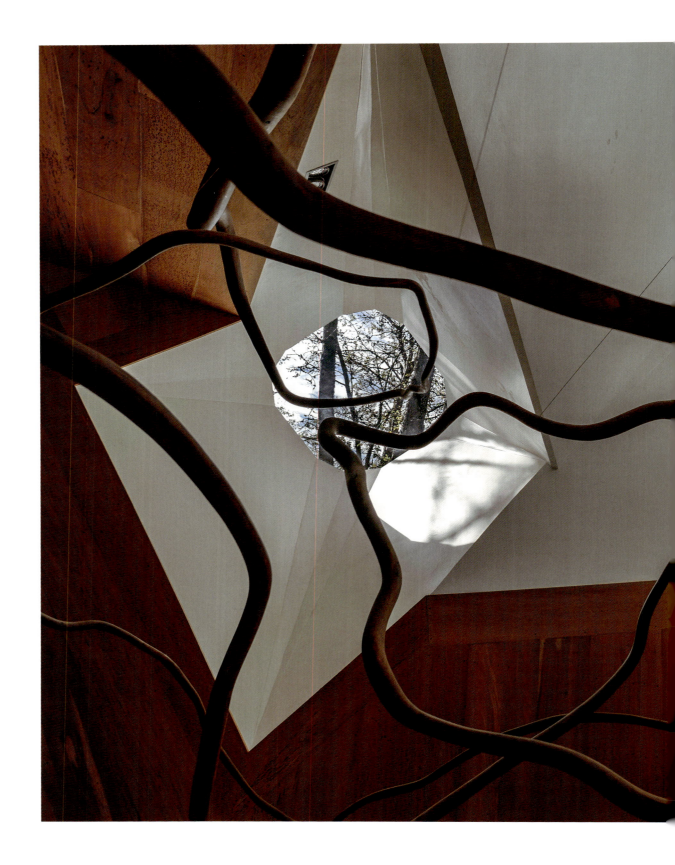

#08

The Boy Hidden in a Fish

2010
12th Venice Architecture Biennale, Italy

For the 2010 Venice Architecture Biennale, just after the earthquake in Chile, we wanted to illustrate a gentle, sheltered, scented future, like the one we found in the dry lines of David Hockney's engraving entitled '*The Boy Hidden in a Fish*'. We chose a 14 t granite boulder at a quarry in the Andes. We drilled it until it was reduced to 7 t in order to facilitate its transport from Chile to Italy, and we placed it in a scented cedar box. The refuge inhabits its interior.

 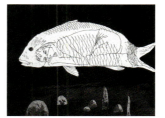

Barnacles　　The Boy Hidden in a Fish, David Hockney

魚に隠れた少年

2010
イタリア、第12回ヴェネチア・ビエンナーレ建築展

チリ大地震の直後に2010年のヴェネチア・ビエンナーレ建築展が開催されたこともあり、穏やかかつ安全で、かぐわしい未来を、ちょうどデイヴィッド・ホックニーがか細い線で描いたリトグラフ「魚に隠れた少年」のようなものを表現したかった。アンデス山脈の採石場に出掛け、重さ14tの巨大な花崗岩をみつくろった。この巨岩を刳り抜き、チリからイタリアへ輸送できるよう重量を7tに減らし、そこへ芳香高いシーダー材の箱を挿入した。内部は隠れ家になる。

PROJECT SKETCH

PROJECT SKETCH

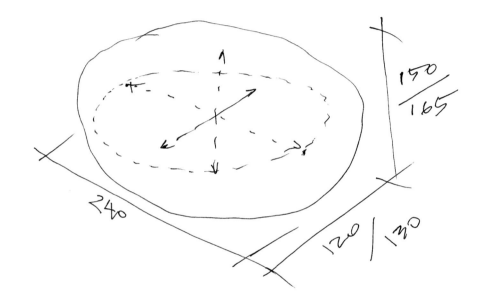

SOLID STONE GRANITE NATURAL
12 TON. APROX.

SKETCH for CONSTRUCTION

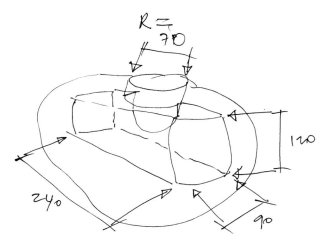

HOLE LESS 7,3 TON APROX.

TOTAL WEIGHT 4,7 TON
MAYBE IN TWO PIECES

PL 2

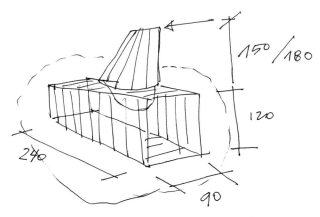

NATURAL WOOD CABIN / BOX
CEDRO WOOD = PERFUME
CIPRES DE LAS
GUAITECAS
WOOD

PL 3

#09

The Boy Hidden in an Egg

2011

The use of literature to imagine architecture is an escapist exercise that often has dire consequences. '*The Boy Hidden in an Egg*' is another engraving in David Hockney's famous 1969 series of illustrations for the Tales of the Brothers Grimm. The design model is a potential 3D illustration of the referenced image, but it is also the starting point for an uncertain project. A cow's udder filled with newspaper and wrapped in wallpaper makes strange movements on account of the structural cables that tie it to the ground.

The Boy Hidden in an Egg, David Hockney

卵に隠れた少年
2011

文学をヒントに建築を着想するというのは、いうなれば現実逃避であり、往々にして悲惨な結果に終わる。「卵に隠れた少年」もやはり、デイヴィッド・ホックニーがグリム兄弟の童話の挿画として制作した1969年の有名な連作リトグラフである。その版画を3次元化したこの模型は、未定のプロジェクトの出発点でもある。雌牛の乳房に新聞紙を詰め、表面に壁紙を貼り付けたものをテンションケーブルで床に固定してみると、奇妙な動きをし始めた。

MODEL with COW'S BREAST by ALEJANDRO LÜER

#10

The Selfish Giant's Castle

2010
Santiago, Chile

We all know that when Oscar Wilde's Selfish Giant returned to his castle, tired after a seven-year absence, he found it had been invaded. He shouted, put up a sign at the entrance and frightened away the children and their constant noise. In retaliation, permanent winter fell upon his garden. Nature made a feast of him until he repented, forcing him to let noise enter his deaf, endearing shelter once again.

  What would the Selfish Giant's castle look like? What would his shelter be like?

わがままな大男の城

2010
チリ、サンティアゴ

お馴染みのオスカー・ワイルドの童話では、わがままな大男が7年ぶりにわが城へ戻ると、留守の間に子供たちが勝手に入り込んでいた。大男は怒鳴り声を上げ、入り口に立て札を立て、騒がしい子供たちを追い払った。ところが大男はその報いを受けたのか、彼の庭だけがずっと冬のままだった。大男が悔い改めるまで、自然は彼を弄ぶ。そしてとうとう、彼が愛着を寄せる音のないシェルターにも子供たちの歓声が戻ってくる。

さて、わがままな大男の城とは、一体どんな建物だろうか。彼のシェルターはどんなだろうか。

PNEUMATICALY MODEL by SMILJAN RADIĆ

PNEUMATICALY MODEL by SMILJAN RADIĆ

FINAL MODEL by SMILJAN RADIĆ

#11

Serpentine Gallery Pavilion 2014

2014
London, England

The *Serpentine 2014 pavilion* is part of the history of small romantic constructions seen in parks or large gardens, the so-called follies, which were hugely popular from the end of the 16th century to the start of the 19th. In general, follies appears as ruins or worn away by time, displaying an extravagant, surprising and often primitive nature. These characteristics artificially dissolve the temporal and physical limits of the constructions themselves with their natural surroundings. These formal mechanisms are taken literally by our pavilion applying a contemporary architectural language. Thus, the unusual shape and sensual qualities of the 2014 pavilion juxtapose with the classical architecture of the Serpentine Gallery to produce a feeling of estrangement in the visitor and an ambiguous relationship between its garden and the new interior we propose.

Today, the folly takes its final position opposite the beautiful gardens designed by Piet Oudolf in the Hauser & Wirth Somerset Foundation in Bruton, England.

Indian Stones

サーペンタイン・ギャラリー・パヴィリオン2014
2014
イギリス、ロンドン

「サーペンタイン・パヴィリオン2014」は、往事は公園や大庭園に置かれていた小さなロマン主義的建造物の、16世紀末から19世紀初頭にかけて人気を博したいわゆるフォリーの流れを汲む。このフォリーはふつう、廃墟というか、いかにも古びた佇まいの、大仰で唐突な存在であり、またしばしば原始的な性格を帯びていたりする。建造物である以上はどうしても時間的・物理的な限界を避けられないから、その限界を自然環境の中で人為的に取り除くためにこうした性格が付与されたのだろう。新パヴィリオンにはこうした形式的手段をそのまま踏襲しつつ、同時代の建築言語を適用することにした。こうして特異な形をした官能的な「パヴィリオン2014」を、新古典様式のサーペンタイン・ギャラリー本館と隣り合わせに並べることで、見学者に違和感を味わわせ、なおかつ新パヴィリオン内部と庭園との関係を曖昧にした。

　現在このフォリーはイギリスのブルートンにあるハウザー&ワース・サマセット財団内に移築されており、その向かいにはピエト・オウドルフの手掛けた美しい庭園がある。

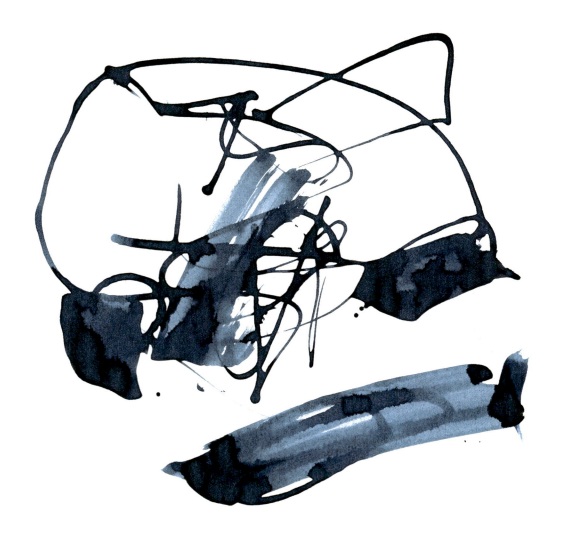

PROJECT SKETCH

PROJECT SKETCH

PROCESS MODEL by YUJI HARADA

PRELIMINARY CLAY MODEL by SMILJAN RADIĆ

FINAL GLASS FIBER MODEL by ALEJANDRO LÜER

GLASS FIBER BUILDING PROCESS

GLASS FIBER BUILDING PROCESS

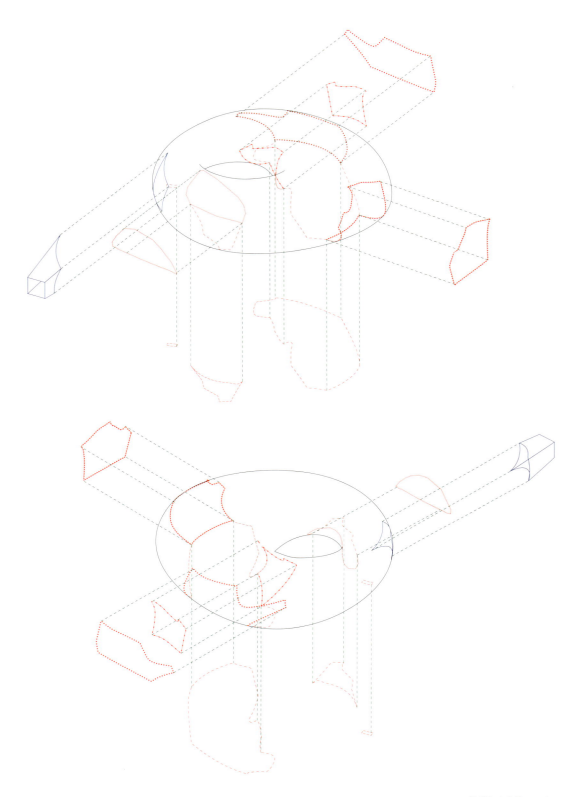

Shell Exploded Isometric

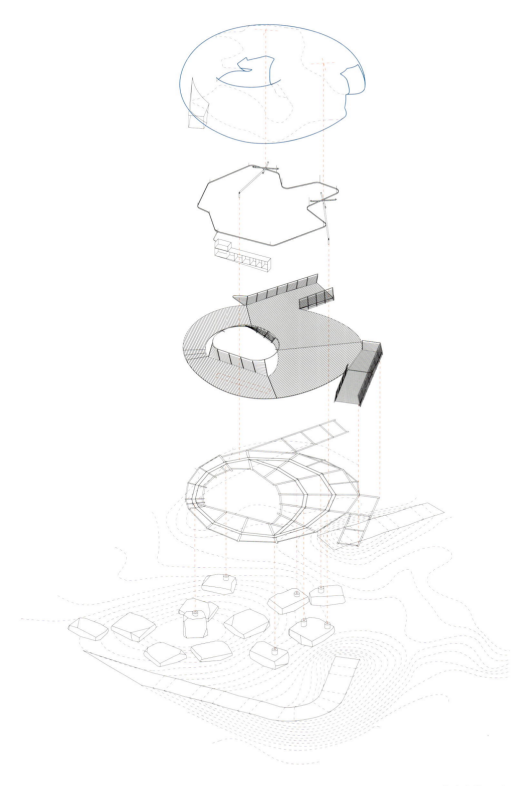

Exploded Isometric

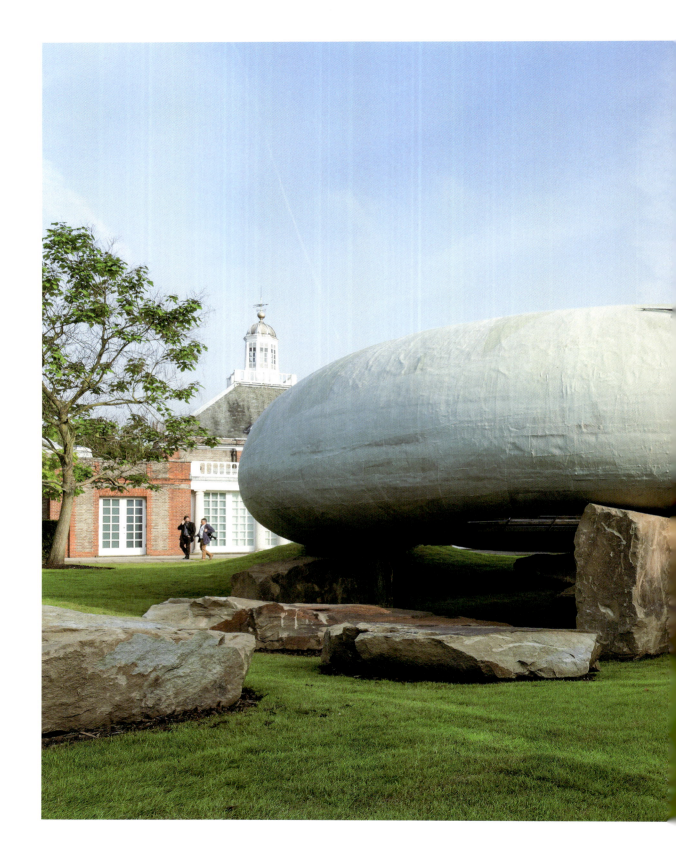

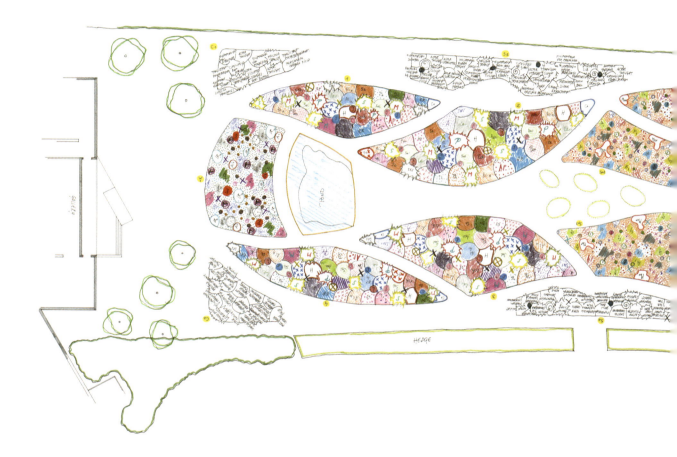

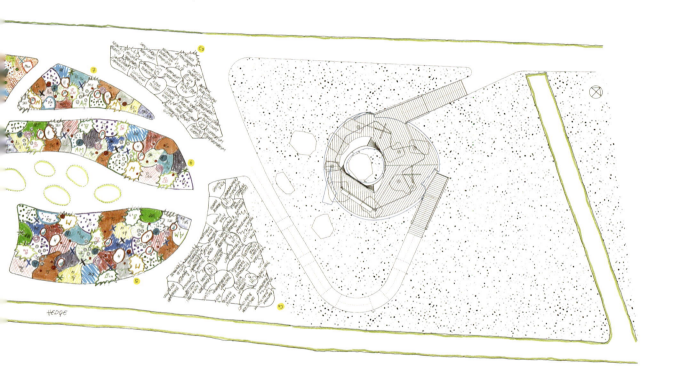

Somerset Plan

HAUSSER and WIRTH SITE PROJECT with PIET OUDOLF GARDEN

Tower
タワー

#12

Santiago Antenna Tower Project

2014
Santiago, Chile

We propose to build a "hybrid" object on the hilltop so that the hilltop maintains its character as a summit and not a saddle. Its appearance wavers between a tower and an antenna: between a stable, recognizable body, and one that dissolves into an unstable apparition. This hybrid is more like a "ghost" than a column. It is the "skeleton" of a ghost of a column. Conceptually, its shape does not propose any novelty for the "future", as its figure is neither clear nor apprehensible at once in the "present". Its reading is sharply confusing. Its form is derived from the recovery of certain works of architecture from the past that interest us… The formal instability of the Tensegrity structures by Buckminster Fuller, the sculptures of Kenneth Snelson, some of the constructivist exercises of Vkuthemas, the polygonal spirals deployed in space by Aleksandr Rodchenko, the handicraft of the Nieuwenhuys Constant tower maquettes, or, more recently, the environment of the Cedric Price Snowdon Aviary in London Zoo, all of them form the real "memory" of this object. We believe that thanks to this retrospective view, —to this apparent "repetition"—, the globalized and diffuse form of this urban object will not be lost to the consumption of a quick "spectacle", nor will it compete with the formal icons built in other cities, something desirable for a Santiago that tries to install its own image in the world.

Nieuwenhuys Constant Portrait

サンティアゴ・アンテナ・タワー計画案
2014
チリ、サンティアゴ

丘の上に〈ハイブリッド〉なオブジェを建てれば、丘の頂上をあくまで頂上として残せるので、頂上を単なる鞍(サドル)代わりにせずに済む。その外観は、タワーとアンテナの間を揺れ動く。すなわち、ある時はいかにも頑丈な躯体に見え、またある時はおぼろに霞んで幻と化す。このハイブリッドは、柱というよりは〈亡霊(ゴースト)〉に近い。さしずめ柱の亡霊の〈骨組み〉といったところだ。この形状は決して〈未来〉指向の斬新さを意図したものではないので、〈今〉の感覚からするとぴんとこないかもしれない。仮にここから何かを読み取ろうとすれば、混乱は深まるばかりだ。実はこの形態は、私たちがこれはと思って掘り起こした過去の建築作品に因んでいる。例えば、いずれも形態の定まらない、バックミンスター・フラーのテンセグリティ構造、ケネス・スネルソンの彫刻、ヴフテマスによるロシア構成主義の試作、アレクサンドル・ロトチェンコが空間に配置した螺旋、コンスタント・A・ニーヴェンホイスの手製したタワー模型、もっと新しいところにセドリック・プライスによるロンドン動物園スノードン禽舎(きんしゃ)の環境などである。いずれも〈記憶〉としてこのオブジェにしっかりと刻まれている。こうして過去——この明らかな〈反復〉——に目を向けたおかげで、たとえこの都市型オブジェが世界的に普及した形式のものであろうと単なる〈スペクタクル〉としてあっさり消費されることもなければ、他都市に建てられたアイコンと競合することもなく、それどころかサンティアゴは自らのイメージを世界に定着させるにふさわしいものをきっと手に入れることになる。

FINAL CARBON FIBER MODEL by ALEJANDRO LÜER

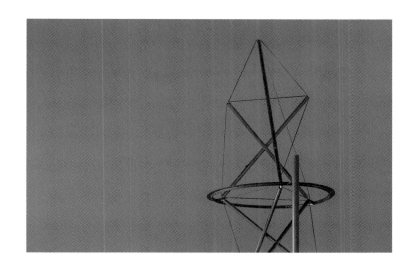
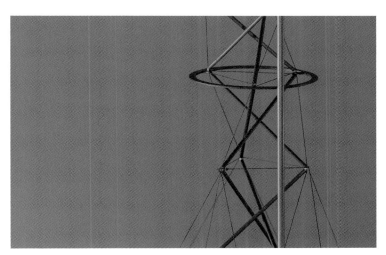

San Cristobal Hill Elevation

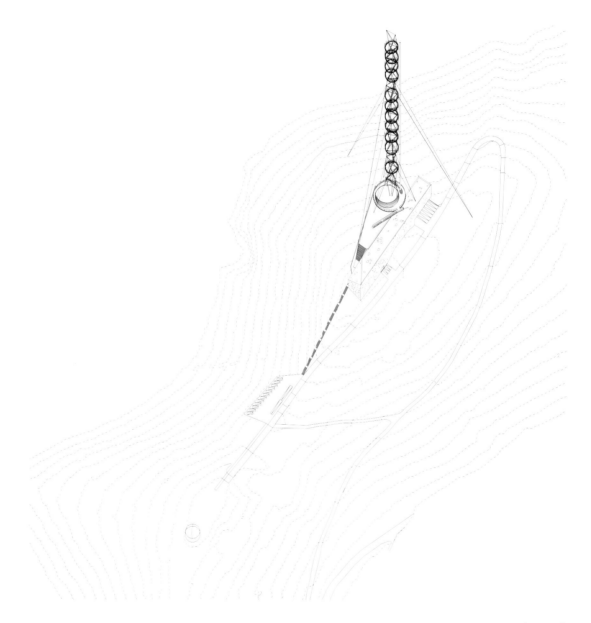

Axonometric

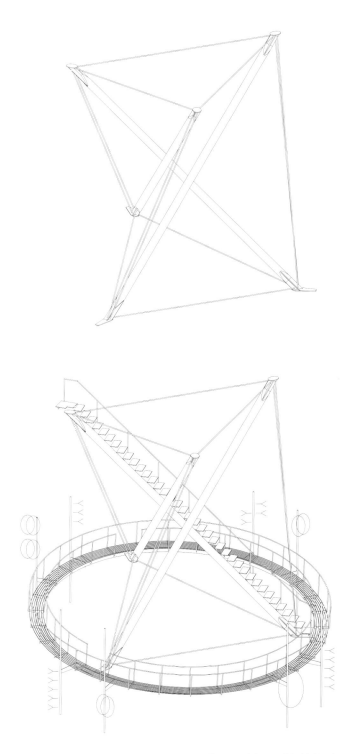

Axonometric Structual Module Detail

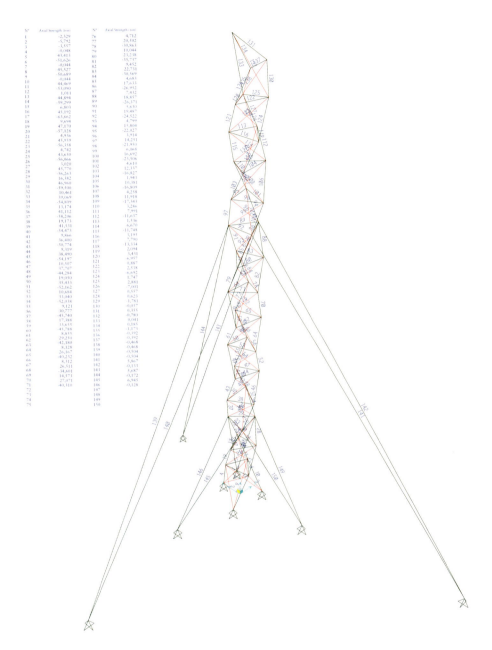

Structural Analysis

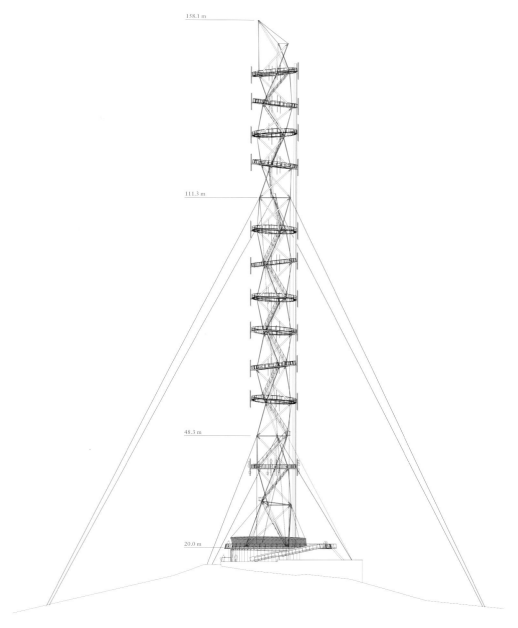

South Elevation

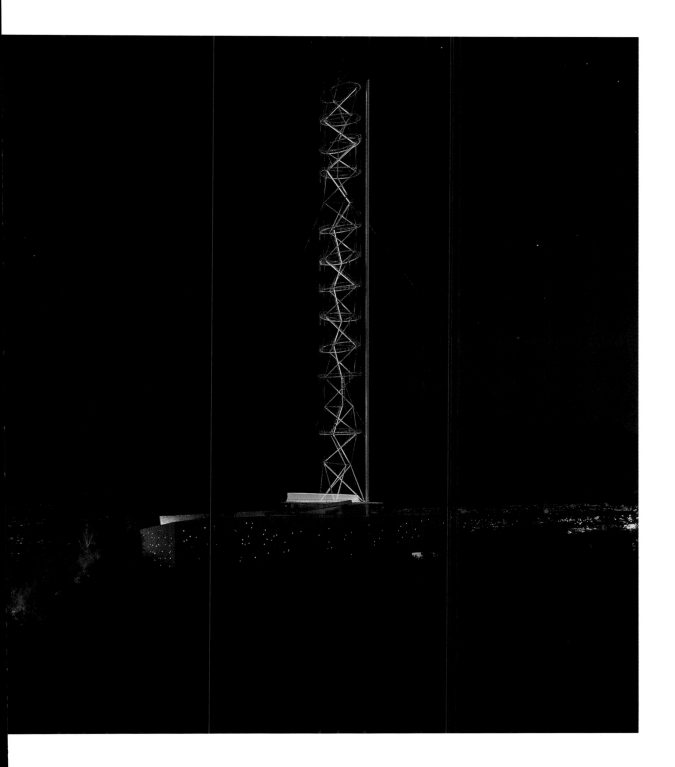

#13

Fragile

2010

Fragile is the name given to a tower of wine glasses that was presented in conjunction with the model of the *House for the Poem of the Right Angle* in 2010 at the 'GLOBAL ENDS' exhibition at the GALLERY·MA in Tokyo. This construction reflects the princess' tower in The Brothers Grimm's fairy tale, 'The Sea Hare', illustrated in a 1969 series of lithograph by David Hockney. This building is a tribute to Constant A. Nieuwenhuys' towers.

The Princess Tower, David Hockney

フラジャイル
2010

「フラジャイル」とは、ワイングラスを塔状に積み上げた作品に付けた名称である。東京のTOTOギャラリー・間で開かれた「グローバル・エンズ」展には、「直角の詩に捧げる家」の模型と併せてこれを出展した。ここでは、1969年にデイヴィッド・ホックニーが連作リトグラフに描いたグリム兄弟の童話『あめふらし』に登場する、王女の暮らす塔を再現した。この建物は、コンスタント・A・ニーヴェンホイスのタワー群へのオマージュである。

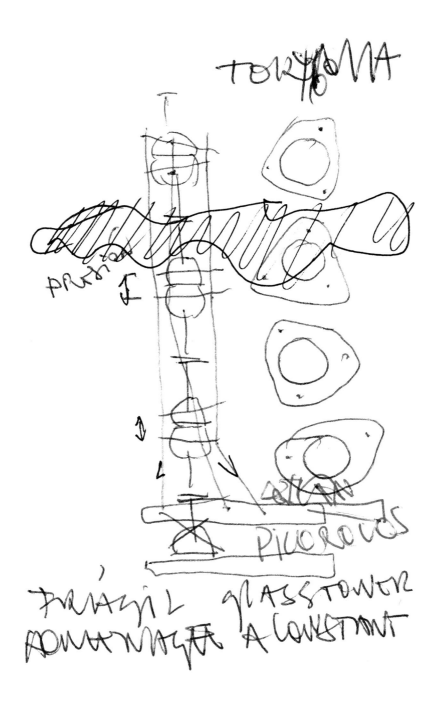

PROJECT SKETCH

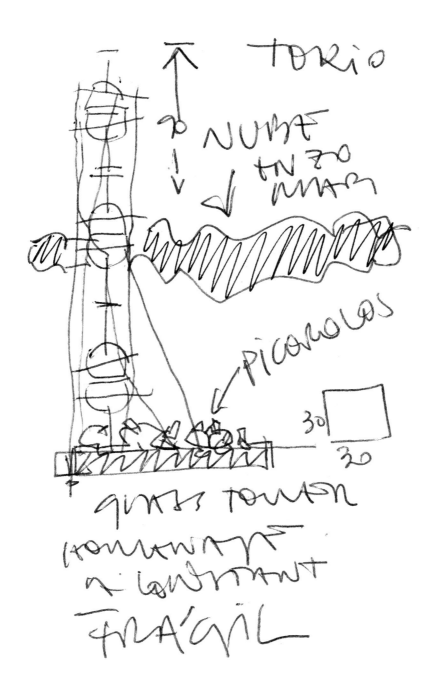

PROJECT SKETCH

#14

Tower Light Bulbs

2015
Santiago, Chile

Tower Light Bulbs is the chance encounter between an old mortar of wood, two useless industrial light bulbs and a cheap Chinese violin parts. All together trying to remember the ghost of a sketch of the *Battersea Power Station*, proposal by Cedric Price in 1984, which I've seen in a beautiful exhibition of drawings of architecture at Hauser & Wirth Somerset in 2015, called 'Land Marks: Structures for a poetic Universe'.

No function, No shape, No drama.

battersea Power Station, Cedric Price

ランプの塔
2015
チリ、サンティアゴ

「ランプの塔」は、古い木製すり鉢、廃品の電球2玉、バイオリンの断片が偶然に出合って生まれた。この組み合わせによって、セドリック・プライスによる1984年のスケッチ「バターシー火力発電所」の亡霊を呼び起こせないだろうかと考えた。私がそのスケッチを目にしたのは、2015年にハウザー&ワース・サマセットで開催された美しい建築ドローイング展「ランド・マーク：詩的宇宙のための構造物」を覗いた時だ。

　機能なし、形なし、ドラマなし。

ALEJANDRO LÜER STUDIO

MODEL with LIGHT BULB by ALEJANDRO LÜER

Stone
石

#15

Mestizo Restaurant

2007
Santiago, Chile

In our initial idea for this restaurant, we created a building with remnants
taken from non-architectural imaginary. In the test model we put together a
children's float, which would be an inflated roof membrane, industrial irrigation
support beams to withstand the lateral compression force, and four granite
blocks weighing 15 t each, used as dead weights to retain this structure and its
possible suction. The whole atmosphere was intended to create a 'pavilion for
estrangement' in the heart of the new park setting, a *Folly*, like the ones that
appear unexpectedly along the hidden side paths in historic parks ... the Chinese,
Japanese or Greek pavilion, the bird pavilion, the pavilion for exotic plants,
butterflies ... The client approved the idea shown in an improvised model, but we
assumed that the local government would not be in favour of a building made
of seemingly ephemeral material, so we changed the technical solution without
abandoning our desire to build a pavilion for estrangement. We designed a
diaphragm of reinforced concrete beams and slabs, rough and painted black,
which generate a pergola or soffit above the park zone designated to the building.
Props descend casually from these beams to granite boulders in different sizes and
weights.

メスチーソ・レストラン

2007
チリ、サンティアゴ

このレストランの当初の発想は、建築とは無縁のイメージの断片を拾い集め、これを建物に仕立てるというものだった。スタディ模型では屋根の張力膜に当たる部分をおもちゃの浮き袋で代用し、また側面からの圧縮力を農業用スプリンクラーの部品を用いた梁で受け、さらにこの構造とその引張り力を保持するための重りとして各15tある花崗岩の塊を4つ置いた。新しい公園の中央にはあえてこの〈異質な雰囲気を漂わせたパヴィリオン〉、すなわちフォリーをつくることにした。ちょうど昔の中国や日本やギリシャにつくられた大庭園で脇道にそれると、ふいに東屋や禽舎、異国の植物や蝶を展示したパヴィリオンなどが姿を現すような感じだ。即興でつくった模型を見て、クライアントはこの案に賛同してくれたが、自治体はまずこの脆い素材で出来た建物を認めてくれないだろうと思ったので、そこは技術でカバーしてあくまでも異質なパヴィリオンを建てるという1点は譲らなかった。そこで剛性を高めるためにざっくりとした黒塗りのRC梁とRCスラブを入れると、これがパーゴラというか軒のように張り出して、ちょうど敷地内の公園指定地域の部分を覆う格好になった。梁から不規則に垂れ下がった支持部材の足元には、大きさも重さもまちまちな花崗岩の塊がある。

CONCEPT MODEL by SMILJAN RADIĆ

PRELIMINARY WOOD MODEL by SMILJAN RADIĆ

FINAL MODEL by GONZALO TORRES

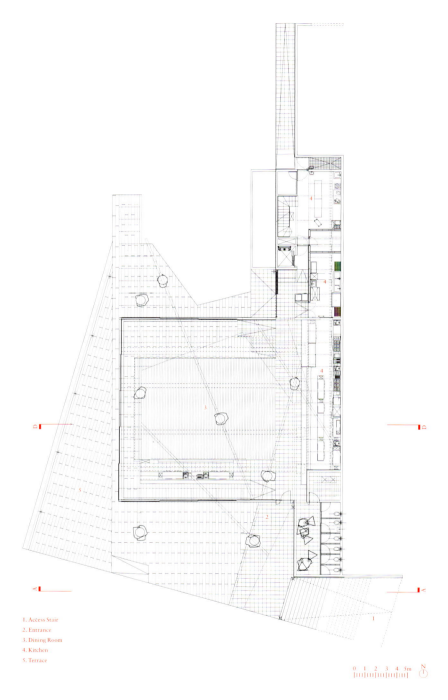

1. Access Stair
2. Entrance
3. Dining Room
4. Kitchen
5. Terrace

Ground Floor Plan

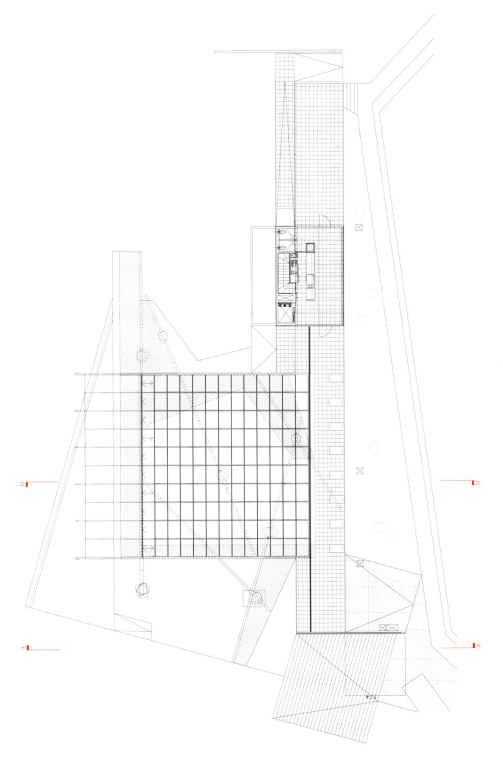

Roof Plan

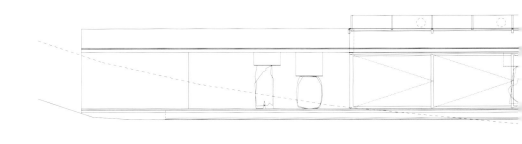
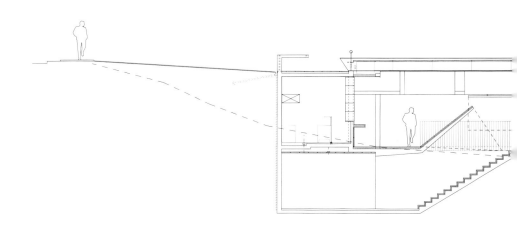
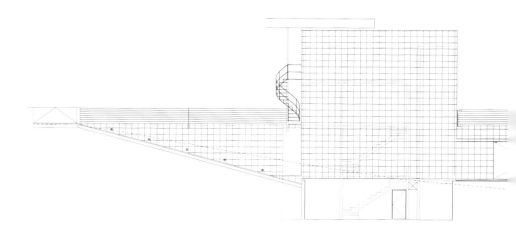

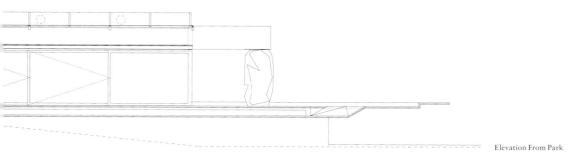

Elevation From Park

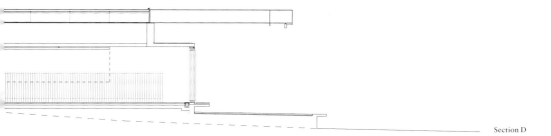

Section D

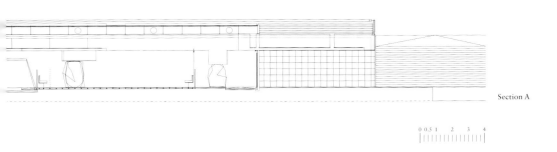

Section A

BUILDING PROCESS

BUILDING PROCESS

#16

Red Stone House

2012
Santiago, Chile

The *Red Stone House* is inserted in a garden with 30m tall trees, planted 40 years ago, a sheltered environment in the heart of the city. In recent times there has been strong development pressure on the neighborhood surrounding the site, and five-story buildings have already appeared not far from here. The owners asked me to build a house for the next thirty years, so the project had to create a domestic interior that would be isolated from these future trends.

The house simply proposes that the users should wander constantly around the garden, as if it were the *Selfish Giant's Castle*: a secret and definitively private space that must be sheltered from the surrounding noise. The interior spaces of the house —split into two wings linked by two long walkways— maintain a homogeneous horizontal level corresponding to the upper elevation of the terrain. Thus, taking advantage of the gentle slope, the face of concrete structure rises naturally from the ground. This simple operation allows the conventional boundaries of the patio at ground level, when seen from the top level, seem to extend beneath the building to the outer extremities of the site, which in turn are treated with shrub vegetation around the perimeters.

Stone Quarry

レッド・ストーン・ハウス
2012
チリ、サンティアゴ

　この住宅が建てられることになった庭は、都心にありながらも、40年前に植えられて今では高さ30mに成長した木々が生い茂っているような閑静な環境にある。近年この付近もついに再開発の圧力に屈したのか、ここからさほど離れていない場所には5階建てのビルもちらほら出現している。30年は保つ家を建ててほしいと家主に言われたので、周辺環境が今後どうなろうとその影響を一切被らないですむよう、独立したインテリアにすることにした。

　テーマは単純で、それは住まい手が家に居ながらにして庭を歩き回れるような住宅、つまり「わがままな大男の城」よろしく、周囲の雑音や騒音を完全に閉ざした秘密の私的空間にするというだけのことだ。住宅——2棟に分割し、その間を2本の廊下で連絡している——内部の床レベルは、敷地の最高地点の高さに揃えた。敷地に緩い勾配がついているおかげで、コンクリート造の建物正面がおのずと地面から持ち上がった形になる。この程度の操作でも、地上レベルにある中庭パティオの印象が変わる。例えば最上階から中庭を見下ろすと、その輪郭が従来の中庭の規格を超えて、建物の足元をくぐり抜けて敷地境界線ぎりぎりまで達しているように見える。かたや敷地境界線については、低木の茂みで覆った。

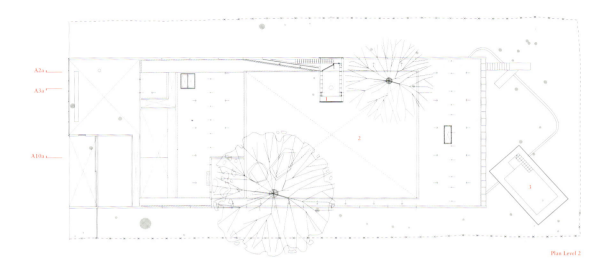

Plan Level 2

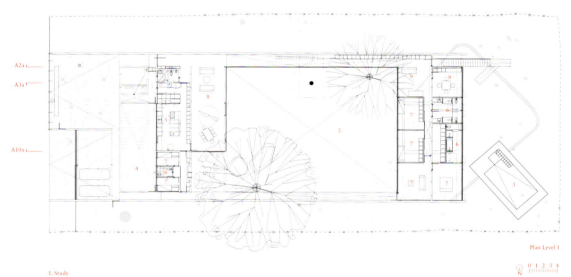

Plan Level 1

1. Study
2. Courtyard
3. Pool
4. Service Courtyard
5. Kitchen
6. Bathroom
7. Bedroom
8. Dining
9. Living

Plans

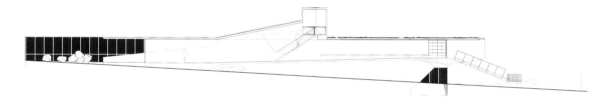

Section A2a

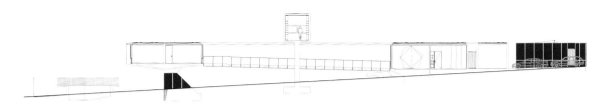

Section A3a

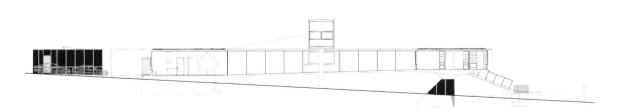

Section A10a

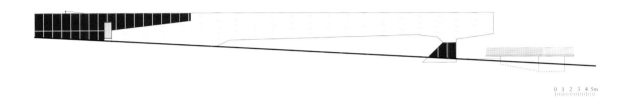

0 1 2 3 4 5m

South Elevation

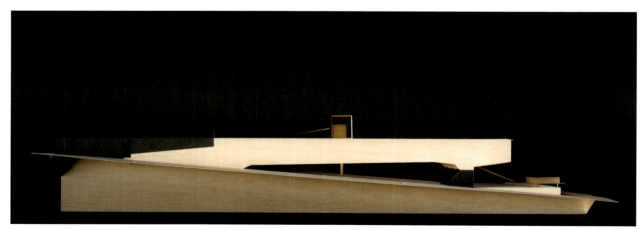

FINAL MODEL by EDUARDO CASTILLO

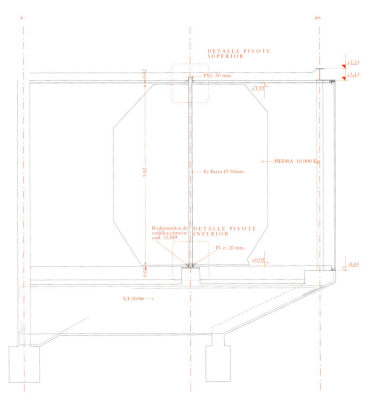

Stone Screen Section Detail

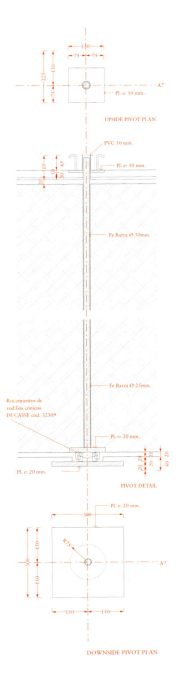

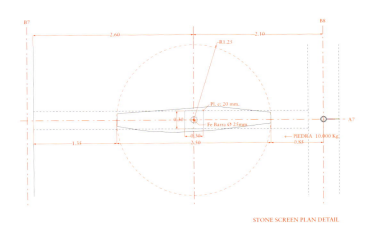

Stone Screen Plan Detail

Downside Pivot Plan

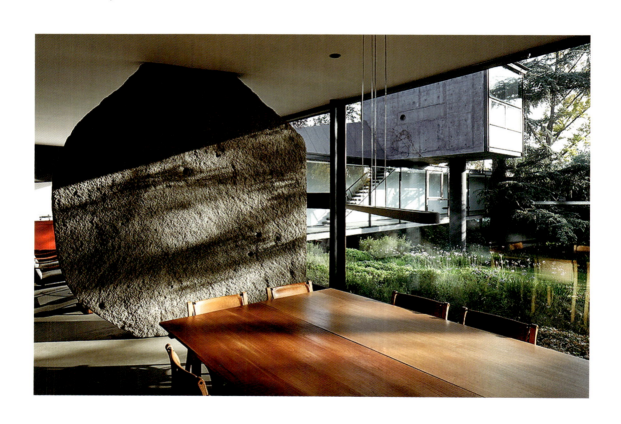

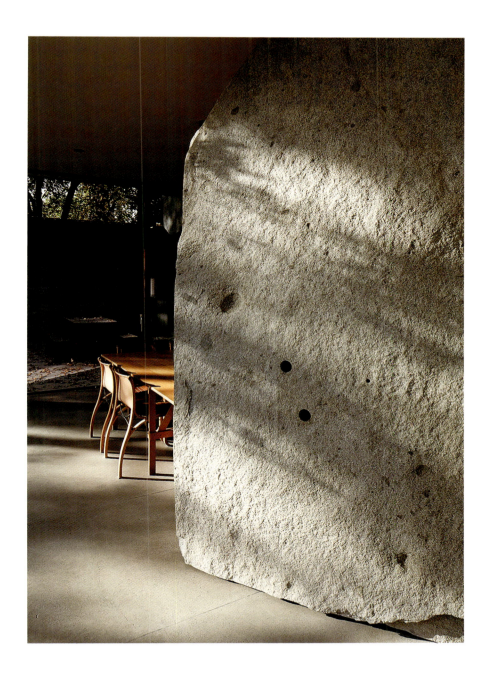

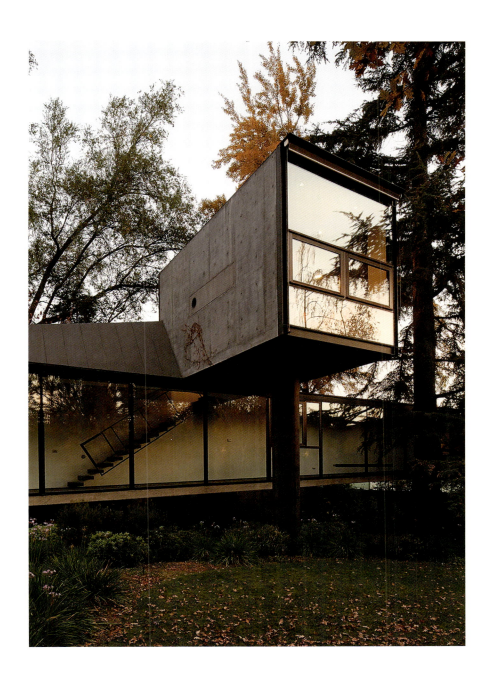

Recent Works
近作

#17

House of Wood

2015
Colico lake, Chile

This house of wood is a weekend residence located by Colico Lake nestled in the commanding mountains and Green that are characteristic of Southern Chile. To be developed in the vast 1 ha graded land rich with trees are two volumes and a platform to match the topography and vista. The 60 m long main building stretches out from the middle of the site in a bridge-like manner, supported by a structure built up vertically, laterally and sideways. The latter structure consists of a combination of modules using 14x14 cm laminated pine joined without any cutting over the pieces.

Sudden Shower over Shin-Ohashi bridge and Atake,
Hiroshige Utagawa

木の家
2015
チリ、コリコ湖

コリコ湖畔に別荘として建てられたこの木造の家は、チリ南部に典型的な見晴らしの良い緑豊かな山間に佇む。木々が鬱蒼と生い茂る1haもの広大な傾斜地に建物のヴォリュームをふたつに分けて建て、さらにデッキを設けることで、この地形と眺望を生かした。敷地中央から全長60mにわたって橋のように浮かんだ母屋を支えるために、その下に支持材を縦横斜めに組んでいる。この支持構造には14cm角のパイン集成材を用いているが、その接合部に当たる木口には一切、細工を施していない。

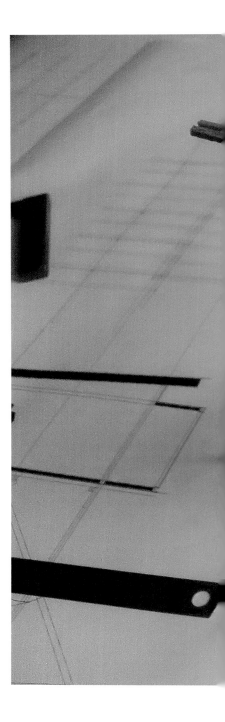

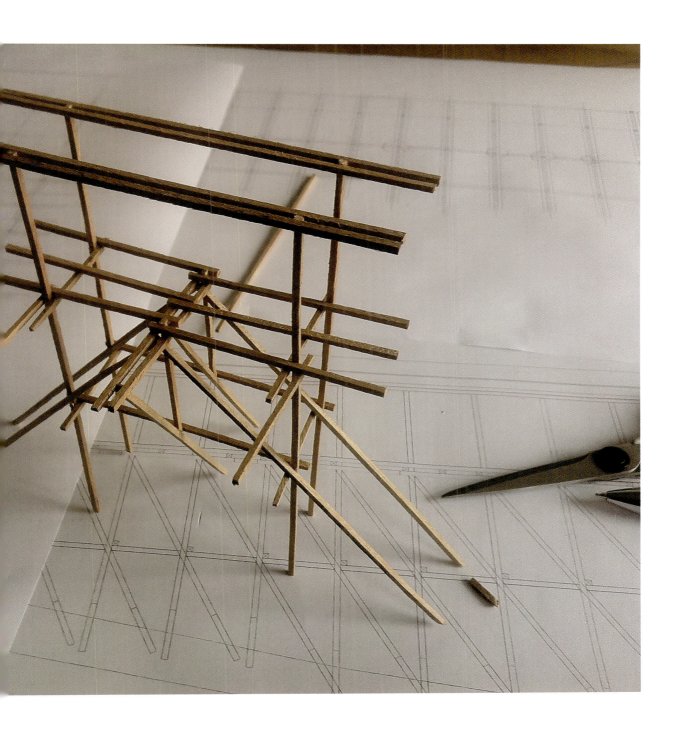

STRUCTURE MODEL by YUJI HARADA

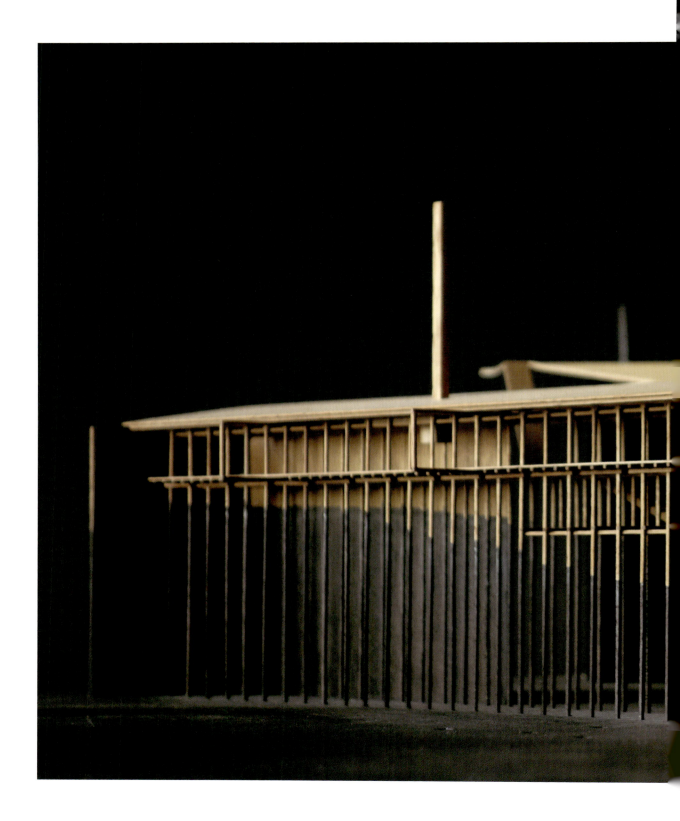

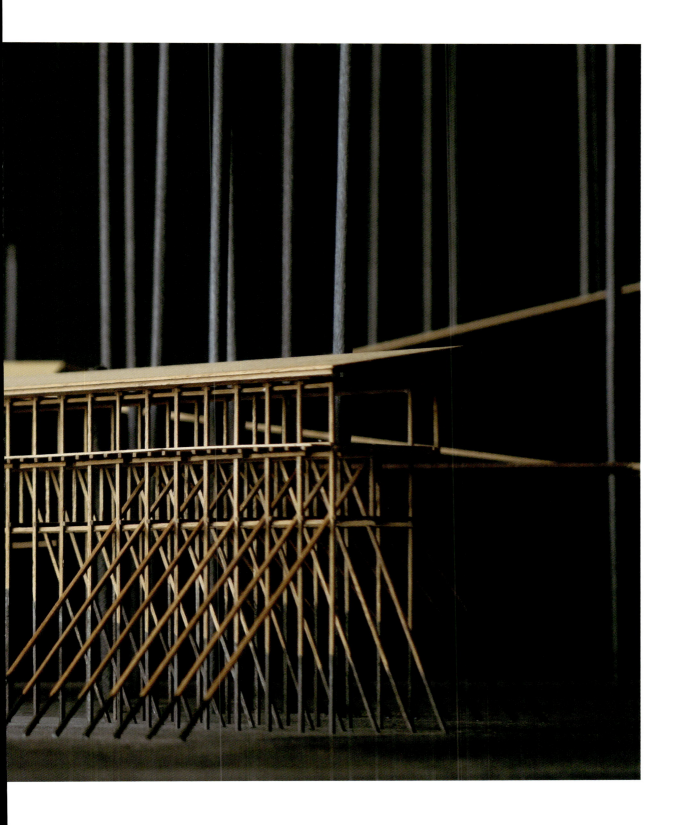

VIIEW by YUJI HARADA

VIEW by YUJI HARADA

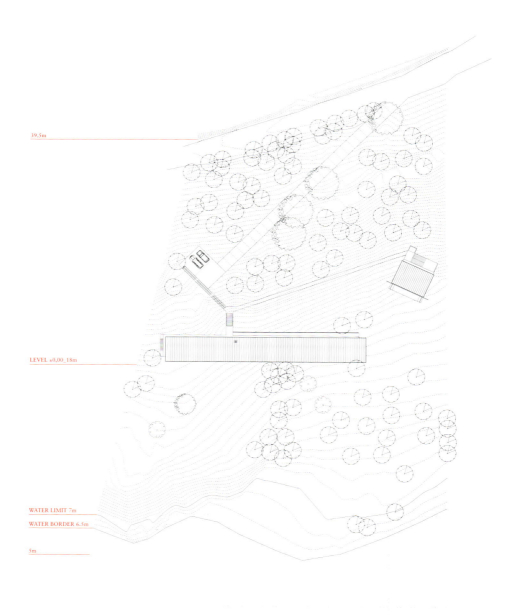

Site Plan

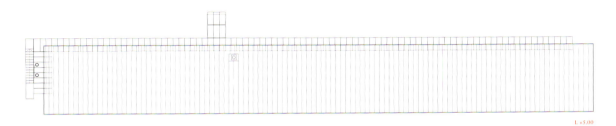

Roof Plan

1. Entrance
2. Kitchen
3. Living Room
4. Bedroom
5. Principal Bedroom
6. Pantry
7. Service Bedroom
8. Warehouse

Floor Plan

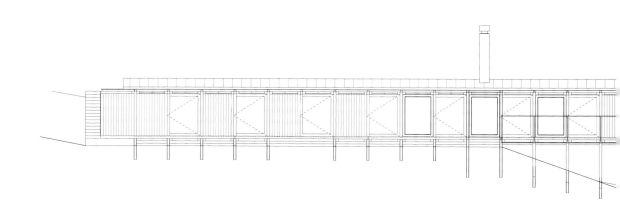

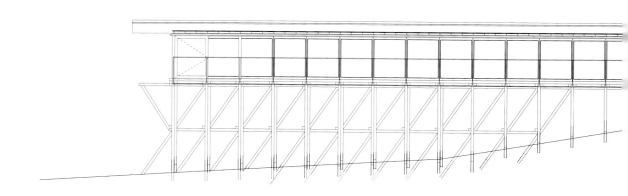

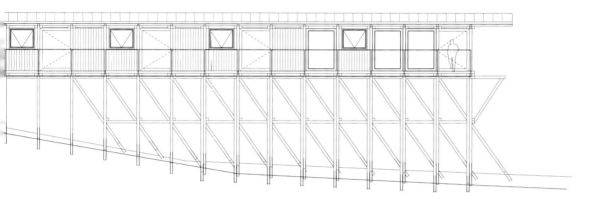

East Elevation

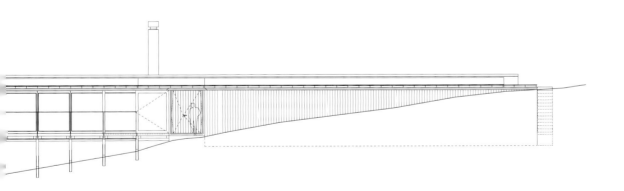

0 1 2 3 4 5m

West Elevation

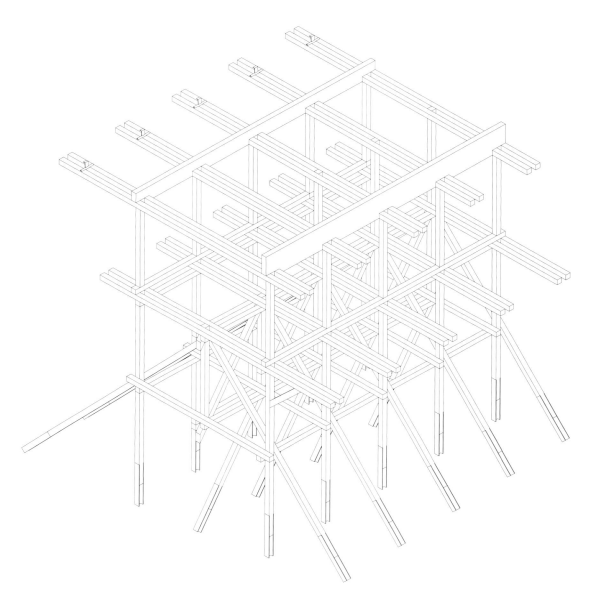

Structural Module Axonometric

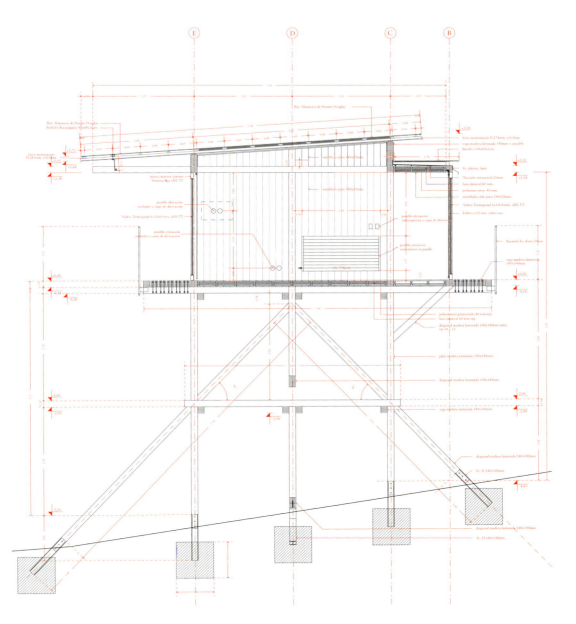

Section Detail

#18

Russo Park Project

2014-
Santiago, Chile

Space made of strips.
The *Russo Park Project* is an events hall located just outside Santiago. It is a simple sun-shade marquee for parties, just like the makeshift structures used for ramadas chilenas, roofs made from palm fronds for public parties, the structure of these shades becomes unstable above our heads. The beams that cross each other 24 or 27 m span are the undeniable focus of the space that is often only covered mechanically. They are held up in the air unstable, supporting a light wooden roof. When they begin to sag, creating tired points, we shore them up with tripods leaving them physically and geometrically embedded. Thus, they return to their useful life, recovering their original form, only to soon begin to lose it to their unstable life. The sagging in the beams produces a predetermined stress even before the arrival of any seismic forces. Thanks to this initial stress, these static deformations are paradoxically more important than those caused by any earthquake.

ルッソ・パーク・プロジェクト

2014-
チリ、サンティアゴ

ストライプの空間

この「ルッソ・パーク・プロジェクト」は、サンティアゴ近郊に建つイベントホールである。パーティー用のシンプルな日除け代わりの大天幕は、ちょうどチリ伝統の祭ラマダに使われる仮設会場の、頭上でゆらゆら揺れるシュロの葉を敷き詰めた屋根のようなものである。ここでは24mないし27mのスパンで交差する梁こそが、まぎれもなく空間の主眼であり、もし梁が露出していない箇所があるとすれば、それは設備機器が取り付けられている箇所に限られる。宙にゆらりと浮いたこの梁が、軽い木造屋根を支える。梁がたわみ始めたら、そのポイントをコンクリートの壁柱と、鉄柱による三脚で支え、そしてこの三脚を物理的にも幾何学的にもそのまま梁に埋め込む。こうして梁は本来の状態に戻り、もとの形状を取り戻すものの、またすぐにたわんで不安定な状態に陥る。この梁のたわみが、地震力が到達しない内から任意の負荷を生じさせる。こうした初期応力のおかげで、皮肉にも地震による変形以上に静的変形の方が顕著になる。

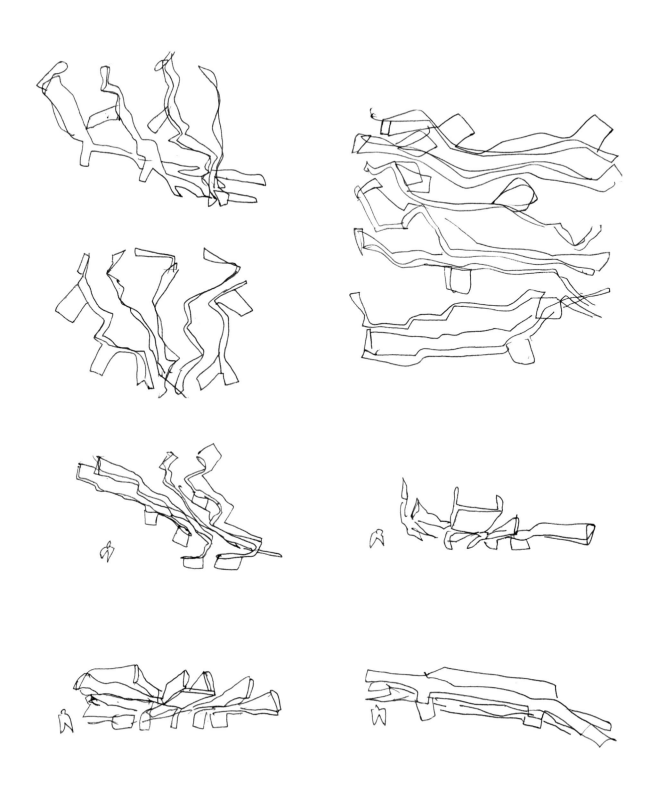

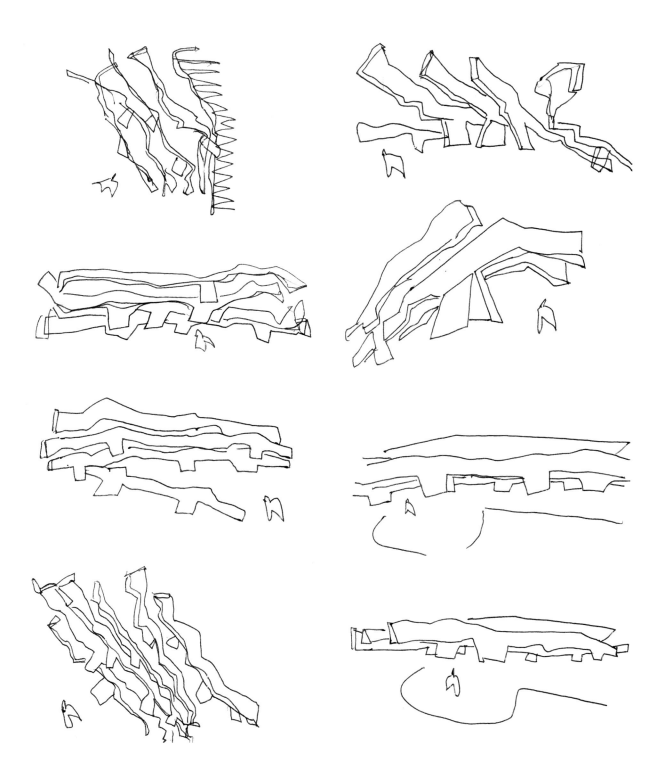

PROJECT SKETCHES

PRELIMINARY CEDAR WOOD MODEL by ALEJANDRO LÜER

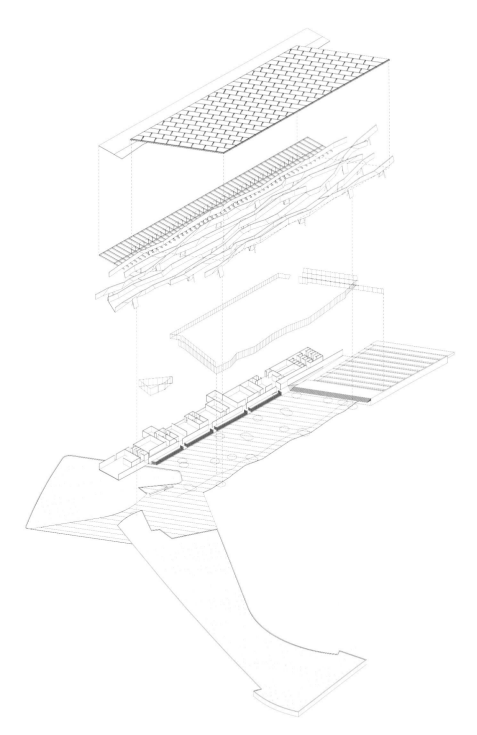

Exploded Isometric

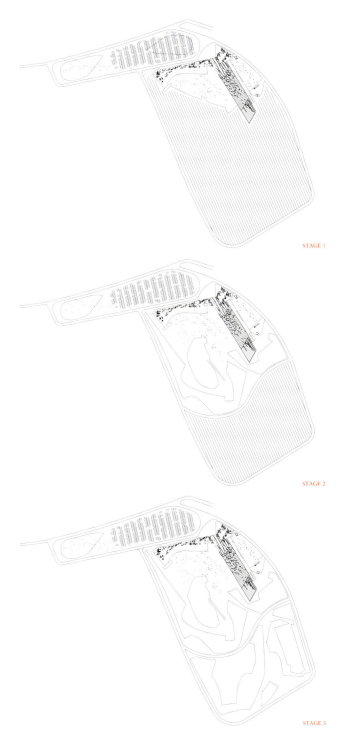

Site Plan, Building Stages

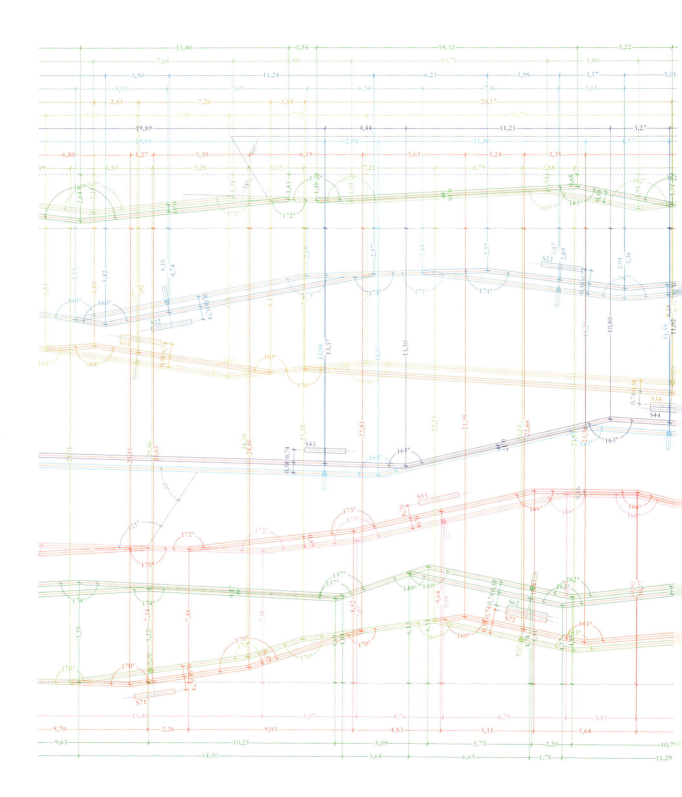

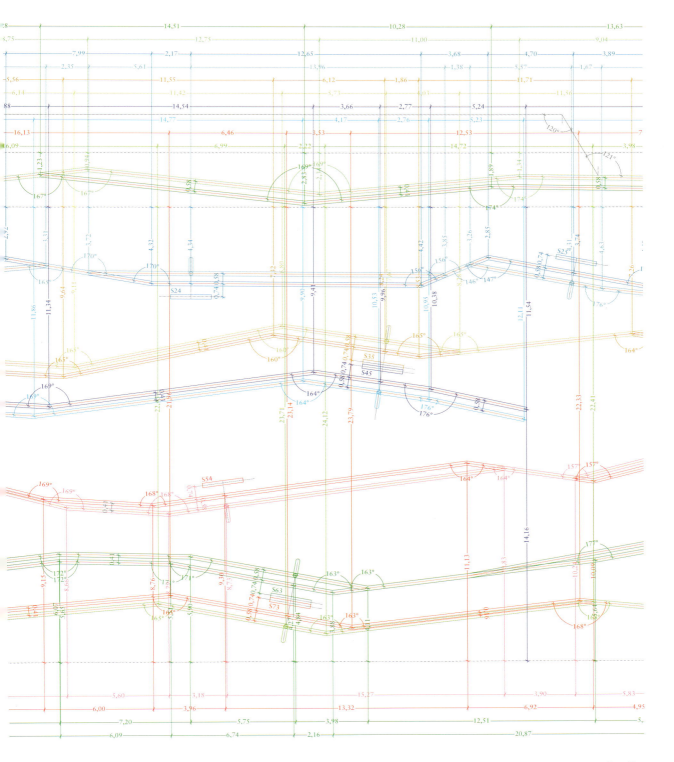

Beam Plan

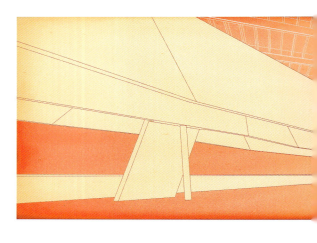
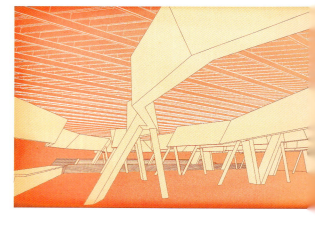

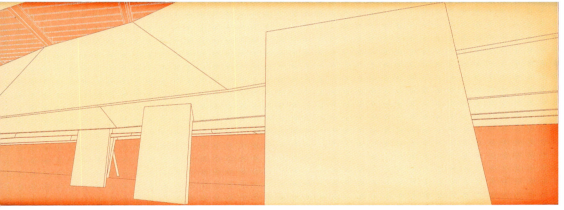

VIEW by YUJI HARADA

Correspondence with Sou Fujimoto_1

TO: Smiljan Radić
FROM: Sou Fujimoto

Dear Smiljan,

A long time has already passed since you took me around to see some of your buildings in Santiago last July. It was a great joy for me to be able to see your body of work and your latest creation, and to get a sense of the atmosphere in your office. I have constantly been stimulated by your work in the past, so having this special opportunity to correspond with you like this is a great pleasure for me. I would like to take this chance to explore the subject of architecture more deeply through your works. After experiencing your Serpentine Gallery Pavilion in 2014, visiting your house and theatre that was near completion in Santiago last year, and examining photographs of your work, I would like to ask you a few questions that came to mind. Although there are actually a multitude of things I would personally like to ask you about your background, your inspiration for pursuing a career as an architect, and the thought process that lies behind specific buildings, I have gradually come up with some questions that are more universal and will also hopefully shed light on the essence of your architecture.

The first one is related to "contemporaneity."

Your architecture has the feel of something that transcends time and has existed since ancient times. This is suggested not only by a straightforward expression of antiquity, such as the use of the huge boulders in the Serpentine Pavilion, but also by the presence of the donut-shaped volume and spatiality that floats above the building. This conveys the sense of an essential space that transcends time or is timeless, and does not belong to any architectural style. I have the feeling that even in a house designed for a contemporary lifestyle, your work is imbued with something that supersedes time. At the same time, your architecture contains an unmistakable contemporaneity. And it seems to me that this is not the contemporaneity based on consumption, but something with a fundamental significance related to the times that we are living in. This is a truly wondrous thing. On the one hand, your work conveys a sense of transcending time or having existed since time immemorial, but on the other, it is unquestionably contemporary. This ambiguity makes your architecture extremely rich and deeply significant. But I am still unable to clearly articulate this quality in your work. What does contemporaneity mean to you? Do you consciously strive for that sort of quality? Or is it something that

藤本壮介との往復書簡_1

TO: スミルハン・ラディック
FROM: 藤本壮介

　　　スミルハンへ

スミルハン、昨年の7月にサンティアゴであなたの設計した建物をいくつか
案内してもらってから、もう随分時間が経ちました。
あなたの実作や最新作に触れ、また事務所の雰囲気を見ることができたことは、
とても大きな喜びでした。以前から僕はあなたの建築に常に刺激を受けてきましたが、
今回、このような往復書簡をやりとりするという、この上ない機会を得られたことは、
僕にとってとても嬉しいことです。あなたの建築を通して、
建築というものをより深く問いかけることができればと願っています。
2014年のあなたの「サーペンタイン・ギャラリー・パヴィリオン」を体験して、
昨年サンティアゴで住宅と竣工間近の劇場（NAVE）に足を運び、また写真を通して
あたなの作品を思考していく過程で、僕の中に浮かんできた問いを、
いくつかあなたにぶつけたいと思います。実際には、生い立ちから、
建築の道に進むことになったきっかけ、また個々の建築の思考のプロセスなど、
個人的に聞いてみたいことは山ほどあるのですが、より一層普遍的で、同時にあなたの建築の
本質をあぶり出すような問いが、徐々に僕の中に湧き上がってきました。

　　　最初の問いは「現代性」ということです。

あなたの建築は、どこか、時間を超越した、太古の昔からそこに存在しているような
雰囲気をもっています。「サーペンタイン・パヴィリオン」での巨石のような、
よりストレートな古代性だけではなく、その上に浮いていたドーナツ型のヴォリュームの
佇まいや空間性にも、どの建築様式にも属さないような、本質的で時間を超えた、
あるいは無時間の場がそこにあるように感じられるのです。
それは現代的な生活を送るための住宅においても、やはりその背後には、
時間を超えた何か、が通底しているように感じられました。
その一方で、僕はあなたの建築は、紛れもない現代性も併せもっていると感じるのです。
消費される現代性ではなく、僕たちが生きているこの時代という本質的な意味においての
現代性が、あなたの建築にはある気がします。しかしこれは、とても不思議なことです。
一方では時間を超えた、太古の時代の存在のような特質が感じられ、また一方では、
それが紛れもなく現代的であるということ。そしてその両義性が、あなたの建築を
とても豊かで意義深いものにしていると思えるのです。
しかしそのあなたの建築がもつ現代性について、僕はまだうまく言葉にできていません。
あなたにとって、現代性とはどのようなものでしょうか？
あなたはそれを意識しているのか？　そもそも現代性など、考えたこともないのか？

Correspondence with Sou Fujimoto_1

never really enters your mind? And how do you see this symbiotic and
reciprocal relationship between timelessness and contemporaneity?

My second question is in one sense linked to the first one, but in another,
something entirely different. It concerns transience and permanence.

As I mentioned, while on the one hand your architecture has the appearance of
something that transcends time and seems to have the potential to remain forever,
you have continued from the beginning of your career to experiment with
temporary buildings. The heir to the tent format that you used in your early houses
can be found in the contrast between the preexisting roof and
the jet-black inner space in your most recent work, Nave.
I was deeply impressed by this fusion and comparison between sensitivity and
intelligence. Similarly, the Serpentine Pavilion, with its extremely thin,
fiber-reinforced plastic, which gently allows the light inside while unexpectedly
shutting out the landscape, seems to be connected to the splendid sensation of
transience in your work. At the same time, the structure and the combination of
the dignified space and materials in your buildings convey an enduring sense of
temporal permanence. What kind of meaning does this fusion of transience
and permanence have for you? Or do you perhaps see these things as
different aspects of the same essence? To me, this ambiguity is
one of the key factors for the diverse and rich nature of your architecture.

My third question is also in one sense linked to the first two, but in another,
something entirely different. It concerns nature and architecture.

While your buildings appear firm within a natural setting, they do not reject nature,
but rather seem to create a gentle link with it. You seem to approach
nature in a more expansive manner that does not simply include greenery and wind,
but also human consciousness and sensations. While at times your buildings
display a strong form, rather than refusing nature, they contain a sense of
generosity regarding the environment and the lives within it. In that respect,
I feel a deep sympathy with your work. But your view of nature seems to differ
in the best sense of the word from my view, which is rooted in the Japanese natural
environment. What do you see as the connection between nature and architecture?
And how do you think the climate and culture of Chile has influenced
or not influenced you?
I can't wait to visit Chile again. Next time I hope I'll have a chance to visit
your villa in Vilches. I'm looking forward to hearing from you soon.

Sincerely,

Sou Fujimoto

藤本壮介との往復書簡 _1

あなた自身の中での、この無時間性と現代性の共存、相互作用は、
どのようなものなのでしょうか？

　　　ふたつ目の問いは、最初の問いと繋がっているとも言えるし、
　　　まったく別のものと捉えることもできます。それは、仮設性と永続性についてです。

上にも書きましたが、あなたの建築には、永遠に続くのではないかと思われる、
時間を超越した佇まいがある一方で、初期の作品から、あなたは仮設的な建築を
試み続けているように見えます。
初期の住宅からで試みられていたテント形式は、最新作である「NAVE」の屋上で
既存部分の漆黒の内部空間との鮮やかな対比として受け継がれています。
この感性と知性が融合した対比の経験に、僕は大きな感銘を受けました。
「サーペンタイン・パヴィリオン」においても、FRPのとても薄い素材が、
柔らかに光を通しながら風景を意外性をもって切り取る様子は、
あなたの素晴らしい仮設性の感覚に繋がるものだと感じます。
その一方で、あなたの建物は、その構成や堂々とした空間と素材の組み合わせによって、
時間の中で生き続ける永続性をももっていると思われるのです。
あなたにとって、この仮設性と永続性の融合とは、いかなる意味をもっているのでしょうか？
それともそれらは異なるように見えて、同じ本質の違った側面なのでしょうか？
僕には、この両義性が、あなたの建築の多様さ、
豊かさを実現している大きな要因のひとつに思えるのです。

　　　3つ目の問いは、これも上のふたつの問いと、繋がっているとも言えるし、
　　　まったく別のものと言うこともできるものです。それは、自然と建築についてです。

あなたの建築は、周囲の自然の中で、確固たる建築であると感じられると同時に、
それは自然を拒否するものではなく、むしろ自然と柔らかく関係を取り結ぶものであるように
感じられます。そしてあなたの建築にとっての自然とは、単に緑や風だけではなく、
人間の意識や感覚をも含めた、より広い意味での自然というものを感じるのです。
あなたの建築が、時に強い形をもちながら、しかし拒絶的ではなく、
むしろ周囲の自然やそこでの生活を対話するようなおおらかさを備えている点に、
僕はとても深く共鳴します。しかしその自然観は、例えば日本の自然の上にある
僕自身の自然観とは、良い意味で異なる気もするのです。
あなたにとって、自然と建築の関係とはどのようなものでしょうか？
そしてその自然とは、チリという風土と文化の中で、あなたにとってどのような影響を与え、
また影響を与えなかったものでしょうか？
またチリを訪れるのを楽しみにしています。次回は、ビルチェスにあるあなたの別荘を、
是非とも訪れたいと願っています。返信を楽しみにしています。

　　　　　　　　　　　　　　　　　　　　　　　　　　　　　藤本壮介

TO: Sou Fujimoto
FROM: Smiljan Radić

Dear Sou,

It really has been a long time. I was hoping to see you in Switzerland at the Beyeler Foundation last month, but the word on the street is that you have designed a watch for women and you were presenting it at the time fair in Basel. Is that right? If so, I'm incredibly envious of your work-rate.

Speaking of watches and time, your questions are very difficult to answer. Contemporaneity is something like a fragile treasure of a work done at just the right moment in history with certain preoccupations floating in the air.

I could answer your first question honestly by saying that I have always tried to make my buildings fit into the history of architecture. More than that, once I finished my education in Chile, I decided to take some courses on the history of architecture at the Instituto Universitario di Architettura di Venezia because I didn't know anything about time in architecture. I travelled to Italy thinking that if I really wanted to make something worthwhile I had to know how buildings were made through history. However, strangely, when I returned to Chile, I became interested in what had been built on the fringes of that great history. I was interested in fragile constructions – things that had no destiny that I could easily find at home and which could not really be called architecture, things that are barely spoken of as constructions.

In the the writer Joseph Brodsky's prologue to Derek Walcott's poem "New World," he wrties, "…*the outskirts are not where the world ends, they are precisely where it begins to unfurl.*" I have used this quote many times at conferences. The world literally unfurls at our borders. After weeks of floating in the sea, things and remnants of things reach our shorelines, bringing news and footprints of faraway lands.

One day, walking on the white sands of a beach on the island of Rapa Nui, a five-hour flight from the continent, I began to gather small, coloured stones of blue, turquoise, grey and orange. I quickly realised that these stones were not stones but actually petrified plastic, worn and cracked with the appearance of stones after the time they had spent floating in the ocean. These bits of plastic had been transformed into SOMETHING, something beyond their origins. I remember I made a necklace for my wife with their remnants, with pieces of oars, pieces of nets and buoys, simple bottle caps and parts of bottles, remnants of remnants.

藤本壮介との往復書簡 _2

TO: 藤本壮介
FROM: スミルハン・ラディック

　　　親愛なる壮へ

すっかりご無沙汰しております。先立ってはてっきりスイスのバイエル財団で
お目にかかれるものと思っておりましたが、噂に聞いたところでは、バーゼル・フェア
(宝飾と時計の見本市)の方で新作の婦人用腕時計を発表なさったとか。
ともあれ、各方面から引っ張りだこのようで、何とも羨ましい限りです。
時計といえば、時間に関するご質問ですけれど、さて何とお答えしたらよいものか。
「現代性」とは、たまたま時代の気運とぴたりと合った作品にごく稀に備わった、
はかないもののような気がします。
　　　　　最初のご質問に正直に答えますと、自分のつくる建物が建築史から
はみ出してはいけない、という意識は常にあります。そういうことでいえば、
私はチリの大学を出てからも、わざわざ建築史を学びにヴェネチア建築大学へ
留学までしています。何しろ建築の時間の流れについては何も知らなかったものですから。
当時はイタリア行きを前にして、もし建築家としてそれなりのものをつくるつもりなら、
建物が歴史を通じてどのようにつくられてきたかを知っておくのは当然のことと
思っておりました。ところがいざ留学を終えてチリへ帰国すると、なぜか偉大な歴史の
片隅に建てられてきたものに興味を覚えたのです。今にも壊れそう構築物は、
何も背負っておらず、建築どころか構築物と呼ぶことすらはばかられるような代物だし、
母国ではとりたてて珍しいものではありませんが、そういうものにおのずと目が向いたのです。
随筆家のヨシフ・ブロツキーが、デレク・ウォルコットの詩『New World』の端書きに
こう書いています。私がよく講演で引用しているものですけれど、
「世界は周縁で終わるのではなく、そこから広がる」。この国境線の向こうには、
文字通り世界が広がっています。海の上を数週間漂ってきた物や破片や残骸が
海岸に打ち上げられ、私たちに遠い地の知らせと痕跡を届けてくれます。
　　　　　いつだったか、南米大陸から飛行機で5時間ほど行った所にある
ラパ・ヌイ(イースター)島の白い砂浜をぶらぶらしながら、足元に転がっていた青や
ターコイズやグレーやオレンジの色あせた小石を拾い集めておりました。
が、見ればそれは小石ではなく、砕けてかちかちになったプラスチック片でした。
海を漂う内に波に揉まれて天然の石のように風化していたのです。
ただのプラスチックのかけらが、素性の知れない〈何か〉に姿を変えていたのです。
たしかこの時見付けたオールや網やブイの屑、瓶のキャップやかけらといった、
いわば残骸のまた残骸を繋いで、妻にネックレスを作ってやりました。
　　　　　この〈何か〉を作品に表現したい、というのが私のかねての思いです。
そうした素性の知れないもの、もしくは独創性に欠けるものにしたくて、
しきりに他人やほかの建築家の先例を参照してきました。

Correspondence with Sou Fujimoto_2

It is that SOMETHING that I have always wanted to appear in my work.
A certain lack of origin or of originality, through a constant reference to others' and
other architects' examples. A deformed and denaturalised reference,
like the denaturalised colour of the plastic remnants I collected on Easter Island.
Since I returned from Italy I have never tried to be true to a grand history of
architecture, of which there are no examples in Chile, but to a history of the
construction we have constantly invented based on the insignificant remnants found
on our own shores.
Perhaps in some of my work contemporaneity is only the ability to know
how to collect and rebuild using these denaturalised remnants.

Permanence

When they asked me to work on the pavilion for the Serpentine Gallery in 2014,
after the appearance of your beautiful cloud in 2013, I felt I didn't have enough tools
to resolve a problem that scared me.
My pavilion is comprised of pieces brought from other places.
Each one proposes a different materiality, but at the same time, time is connected to
the materiality and its shapes, making a hybrid object. It is an object that points in
many ways at the same time. The model I used for the project had been created
three years before in reference to the story "The Selfish Giant" by Oscar Wilde.
It is made completely out of papier mâché. Everything is resolved in one go,
the entire single-material shell. This synthesis does not occur with the final pavilion.
On the other hand, as I see it, my pavilion felt comfortable in that English setting
unlike your extremely synthetic cloud from the previous year in the same place.
Your project was able to get to the bones of architecture. Leaving it naked,
it was able to say: THIS IS IT. That capacity for synthesis is completely elusive to me.
Only once have I tried to synthesise a project in that way, without much success.
It was one of the first refuges I called a "Room."
That capacity for *synthesis* (though that is not quite the right word) can
be found in almost all of Christian Kerez's projects, with his close ties to Japanese
architecture through his admiration of Shinohara, especially in his exquisite
house with one wall. And we can also find it in the incredible Teshima Art Museum
by Ryue Nishizawa, perhaps the most moving building that I have ever been in,
after Le Corbusier's Palace of Assembly in Chandigarh. These two projects, by Kerez
and Nishizawa, have something precise. They appear to be born from a luminous
idea outside reason. Their appearance is so decisive that it seems as if there was no
prior project stage, just the unfurling of ideas. They appear to have been made to
last forever.
This power of synthesis is not available to me. In my projects, I tend to cram
things together, to assemble, and to give a time or historical place to the chosen
parts, so that when they are put together in a single project, they can convey another
history. Not a new history of architecture, but another history.

ただしその先例が作品の中では本来の性質も原形もとどめていないところは、
イースター島で拾った色あせたプラスチック片と似たようなものです。
イタリアから戻ってからというものは、偉大な建築史に忠実であろうとするのはやめました。
第一、チリにはそのお手本自体がありませんし。代わりに建設の歴史に忠実であるために、
チリの浜辺に打ち上げられたちっぽけなかけらを用いて、毎回一から自力で
つくり上げることにしたのです。

　　　　もし私の作品に現代性があるとすれば、それは、色あせたかけらを拾い集めて
それを再構築するという感性でしょうか。

　　　永続性

2014年にサーペンタイン・ギャラリーのパヴィリオン設計の依頼を受けましたが、
何しろその前年にあなたのあの美しい雲を拝見したばかりでしたから、
こんな難問を解くには自分は役不足だ、とすっかり怖じ気付いてしまいました。
　　　　結局私は、方々から部品を集めてパヴィリオンをつくりました。部品一つひとつは
素材が異なりますが、質感と形の隔たりは時間が埋めてくれるので、全体としては
ハイブリッドなオブジェになっています。多くの暗示を含んだオブジェというか。
このプロジェクトの原型となったのが、その3年前にオスカー・ワイルドの
「わがままな大男の城」にちなんで制作した模型です。模型の材料は紙粘土なので、
こねるだけで形が決まります。ところが現実のパヴィリオンは、そんなにうまく
まとまってくれません。私の見る限り、前年に同じ場所にあなたが多様なものを
ある概念のもとに統一してつくった、非常に統合的な雲とは異なり、わがパヴィリオンは
英国の環境にすっかりくつろいでいるようでした。一方あなたは建築を極限まで削ぎ落とし
丸裸にして、「こういうことですよ」といわんばかりに差し出した。一体どのようにして
あれほど多くの部材をまとめ上げているのか、私には皆目見当が付きません。
一度だけそうした統合的なプロジェクトを試みたことがありますが、うまくいきませんでした。
隠れ家シリーズの初期作「ルーム」のことですが。
　　　　統合体（どうもしっくりこない言葉ですが）といえば、クリスチャン・ケレツの作品の
ほとんどがそうです。もともと篠原一男を崇拝していた彼の作品には当然ながら日本建築に
通ずるものがあって、そのことはあの端整な「壁一枚の家」によく現れています。
それから西沢立衛の傑作「豊島美術館」もそうで、実際に訪れてみると、個人的には
ル・コルビュジエの「チャンディーガルの国会議事堂」以来の感動を覚えました。
ケレツと西沢の両作品には何と言うか、無駄がありません。何か理屈を超えた、
ひらめきから生まれたようにも見えます。およそ迷いがなく、いきなりそこに
到達してしまったというか、思い付くままに進めていったらそうなったという感じです。
永遠にそこに存在するべくしてつくられたようにも見えます。
　　　　これだけのものをまとめ上げる力は自分にはありません。私はどちらかと言うと
あれもこれもと詰め込むタイプで、その中の特定のものにだけ過去の時間や場所を
仕込んでおいて、プロジェクトにもうひとつの歴史を語らせます。建築史に新たな局面を

In this way, my architecture is old and doddering. For example, I tried to insert the pavilion at the Serpentine Gallery into the history of architecture as a folly. Not as a contemporary view of what could be – a capricious pavilion in a park – but rather a historical view, a romantic one, where you don't know what is real and what is false, what is support and what is dressing, what in the end is permanent and what is ephemeral, current or past, serious or humorous, as Cedric Price said.

3. Nature and Architecture

This year I went back to teaching architecture classes. It had been a long time since I'd been in contact with young people. The first semester we are doing a workshop with my friend Alberto Sato and Gabriela Villalobos in Chile, and in the second semester I am hoping to work with Christian Kerez in Switzerland, another island, just like Chile and Japan, according to Hans Ulrich Obrist. Our workshop is called "Replica of the Invention of Chile" and it involves creating a guide to contemporary construction in Chile. Before we set foot in these lands, their nature and distance were invented, inventing the end of the world. *The Invention of Chile* confirms that the natural elements in the land are a construction, a narrative. Thus, truly wild nature does not exist.

This book on the territory contains nature at the end of the world. It is potent, inhospitable. The important aspect is that it is something that must be explored and by exploring it, you face it on equal terms. My grandfather was Croatian and he arrived in the Chilean desert to work in the nitrate mines in 1919. For an immigrant at that time, nature was not something to be explored but rather a resource. Something close at hand and something to converse with. It is something we could live with without guilt. But for an immigrant, that dialogue was based on memories and recollections that survived in him through his journey, memories that were born in other places. The combination of his foreign memory and his immediate needs for subsistence often made his way of acting or relating to the world appear more coarse and functional, less simple or primary... more tactile.

I would like something of that old immigrant's way of acting to appear in my work – to converse on equal terms with nature as an explorer would, and in order to survive, do as little damage as possible.

Smiljan Radić

付け加えるというのではなく、まったく別の歴史を一から編むのです。
われながらずいぶんと古くさい建築をつくっているものです。
例えばサーペンタイン・ギャラリーのパヴィリオンについては、これを建築史の〈フォリー〉の
項目に付け加えるつもりでした。現代的な視点からすれば、公園の中に奇抜なパヴィリオンを
つくることになるのでしょうが、そうではなく、かつてのロマン主義的な視点で、
虚実がないまぜになったものを、あるいは、どれが土台でどれが仕上げか、どれが最終的に
残るか残らないのか、何が現在のもので過去のものか、セドリック・プライス風に言えば、
まじめなのかふざけているのか、分からないものをつくることにしたのです。

3. 自然と建築

今年は大学へ戻って建築学部生を指導しました。若者と接するのは久しぶりのことです。
前期のワークショップは、チリ在住の友人アルベルト・サトウとガブリエラ・ビリャロボスに
手伝ってもらったので、後期はスイスからクリスチャン・ケレツを呼ぶつもりです。
ハンス・ウルリヒ・オブリストに言わせると、スイスもチリや日本と同様に
〈島国〉だそうですから。ワークショップでは〈『チリの発明』のレプリカ〉と題して、
チリの現代構築物のガイドブックを作成しています。われわれがこの国の土を踏む以前に、
その自然と距離が発明され、世界の果てが発明されました。『チリの発明』が述べるように、
この土地にもともとあった自然なものとはすなわち、構築物であり、物語なのです。
だから、まったく手付かずの自然など存在しません。
　このガイドブックには、世界の果ての自然が紹介されています。人を寄せ付けない、
強大な自然が。重要な点は、それが調査されるべき対象であり、そして調査をする側は、
それと対等な立場で向き合うことになります。ところでクロアチア人だった私の祖父は
1919年にチリに渡り、砂漠の中の硝酸塩鉱山で働きました。当時の移民にとって自然は
調査の対象ではなく、単なる資源でした。身近にあって、気兼ねなく付き合える
話し相手というか。ところが移民の場合、ふるさとの思い出を胸にはるばるよその土地に
来ていますから、自然と対話をする場合にも、どうしてもそうした記憶を頼りに
してしまいます。ふるさとの記憶が染み付いたまま、生活の糧を得るためによその地に
暮らしているせいか、世界の捉え方、世界との付き合い方がどうしても荒っぽく、
実際的になります。素直でないというか……皮膚感覚が優先されるのです。
　私はこの老移民の振る舞いを、いくらか作品に反映させ――一調査者のように
自然と対等に付き合えるようにさせたい、逆に自分が生き延びるために
自然を破壊するような真似はさせたくないのです。

スミルハン・ラディック

Project Data

#01
NAVE, Performing Arts Hall
Site: Santiago, Chile
Design period: 2010-2015
Construction period: 2010-2015
Site area: 1,270 m²
Construction area: 1,770 m²
Architects: Smiljan Radić
Model: Alejandro Lüer
Collaborators: Eduardo Castillo, Danilo Lazcano,
Patricio Alvarado
Structural engineers: BYB ingeniería Estructural Ltda.
Structural system: Reinforced Concrete

#02
Room
Site: Chiloé Island, Chile
Design period:1992-2007
Construction period: 1991-2007
Site area: 54ha
Construction area: 150 m²
Architects: Smiljan Radić
Model: Smiljan Radić
Collaborators: Ricardo Serpell, Felipe Montegu
Structural system: Wood, Polyester membrane/PVC

#03
Bío Bío Regional Theatre
Site: Concepción, Chile
Design period: 2011-2013
Construction period: 2015-
Site area: 19,880 m²
Construction area: 3,525 m²
Architects: Smiljan Radić, Eduardo Castillo,
Gabriela Medrano
Model: Alejandro Lüer
Collaborators: Danilo Lazcano, Gonzalo Torres,
Yuji Harada, Andres Battle (images)
Structural engineers: BYB ingeniería Estructural Ltda.
Structural system: Hormigón armado, madera,
membrana PTFE

#04
Chilean Museum of Pre-Columbia Art Extensions
Site: Santiago, Chile
Design period: 2008-2014
Construction period: 2011-2014
Site area: 4,140 m²
Construction area: 3,056 m²
Architects: Smiljan Radić
Model: Alejandro Lüer
Collaborators: Eduardo Castillo, Danilo Lazcano,
Loreto Lyon, Patricio Alvarado
Structural engineers: BYB ingeniería Estructural Ltda.
Structural system: Reinforced Concrete,
Membrane ETFE

#05
Meeting Point
Site: Without place
Design period: 2009
Construction period: 2009
Construction area: 190 m²
Architects: Smiljan Radić, Gonzalo Puga (designer),
Osvaldo Sotomayor (architect)
Model: Alejandro Lüer
Collaborators: Patricio Alvarado
Structural engineers: Santiago Arias
Structural system: Membrane ETFE / Polyester PVC,
Basalt, Steel.

#06
Environmental Science
Museum Guadalajara Project
Site: Guadalajara, Jalisco, Mexico
Design period: 2011
Site area: 13,000 m²
Construction area: 5,470 m²
Architects: Smiljan Radić, Eduardo Castillo
Model: Alejandro Lüer
Collaborators: Gonzalo Torres, Matías Zegers,
Christian Juica, Nicolás Norero
Mechanical engineers: Manuel Gutiérrez
Structural system: Reinforced Concrete,
ETFE Membrane, Brick

#7
House for the Poem of the Right Angle
Site: Vilches, Chile
Design period: 2010-2011
Construction period: 2011-2012
Site area: 4.5 ha
Construction area: 165 m²
Architects: Smiljan Radić
Landscape: Marcela Correa (sculptor)
Model: Alejandro Lüer
Collaborators: Jean Petitpas
Structural engineers: Pedro Bartolomé
Structural system: Reinforced Concrete

#08
The Boy Hidden in a Fish
Site: Venecia, Italia,
The Coederie Bienal of Architecture of Venecia, 2010
Design period: 2010
Construction period: 2010
Construction area: 4 m²
Architects: Smiljan Radić, Marcela Correa (sculptor)
Model: Smiljan Radić
Collaborators: Sergio Rivas, Juan Araya,
Marcelino López, Gerardo Rojas, Juan Castillo
Structural system: Granite, Wood

#09
The Boy Hidden in an Egg

Design period: 2011
Architects: Smiljan Radić
Model: Alejandro Lüer
Structural system: Cow udder, Stainless Steel, Wood

#10
The Selfish Giant's Castle

Design period: 2010
Architects: Smiljan Radić
Model: Alejandro Lüer
Structural system: Paper mache

#11
Serpentine Gallery Pavilion 2014

Site: London, England
Design period: 2013-2014
Construction period: 2014
Site area: 1,610 m²
Construction area: 201 m²
Architects: Smiljan Radić
Model: Alejandro Lüer
Collaborators: Yuji Harada, Claudio Torres,
Gabriela Medrano
Structural engineers: David Glover, Thomas Webster,
Jack Wilshaw, Katja Leszczynska, Brian Graham
Structural system: Fiber Glass, Natural Stone, Steel

#12
Santiago Antenna Tower Project

Site: Santiago, Chile
Design period: 2014
Site area: 8,000 m²
Construction area: 3,895 m²
Architects: Smiljan Radić, Gabriela Medrano,
Ricardo Serpell
Model: Alejandro Lüer
Collaborators: Claudio Torres, Matiaz Valcarce
Structural engineers: BYB ingeniería Estructural Ltda.
Structural system: Steel, Concrete

#13
Fragile

Design period: 2010
Construction period: 2010
Architects: Smiljan Radić
Model: Alejandro Lüer
Collaborators: Patricio Alvarado
Structural system: Wine glass, Stainless Steel, Wood

#14

Tower Light Bulbs

Design period: 2015
Construction period: 2015
Architects: Smiljan Radić
Model: Alejandro Lüer
Structural system: Violin, Lamp, Wood

#15
Mestizo Restaurant

Site: Santiago, Chile
Design period: 2005-2007
Construction period: 2005-2007
Construction area: 652 m²
Architects: Smiljan Radić
Collaborators: Marcela Correa (sculpture),
Danilo Lazcano, Cristóbal Tirado, Gonzalo Torres
Structural engineers: Luis Soler y Asociados
Structural system: Reinfoced Concrete, Natural Granite

#16
Red Stone House

Site : Santiago, Chile
Design period: 2009-2012
Construction period: 2011-2012
Site area: 2,200 m²
Construction area: 565 m²
Architects: Smiljan Radić
Collaborators: Marcela Correa (sculpture),
Eduardo Castillo, Patricio Alvarado
Structural engineers: BYB ingeniería Estructural Ltda.
Structural system: Reinfoced Concrete

#17
House of Wood

Site: Colico Lake, Chile
Design period: 2013-2015
Construction period: 2013-2015
Site area: 10,000 m²
Construction area: 420 m²
Architects: Smiljan Radić
Model: Alejandro Lüer
Collaborators: Danilo Lazcano, Yuji Harada
Structural engineers: BYB ingeniería Estructural Ltda.
Structural system: Wood

#18
Russo Park Project

Site: Santiago, Chile
Design period: 2015-
Site area: 1,370,000 m²
Construction area: 5,770 m²
Architects: Smiljan Radić
Model: Alejandro Lüer
Collaborators: Yuji Harada, Gabriela Medrano
Structural engineers: BYB ingeniería Estructural Ltda.
Structural system: Reinforced Concrete, Wood, Brick

Credit

Japanese translation
和訳

Jun Doi
土居 純
p. 5, p. 11, p. 35, p. 53, p. 73, p. 95, p. 105, p. 119,
p. 141, p. 151, p. 155, p. 161, p. 187, p. 201, p. 207,
p. 215, p. 239, p. 259, p. 285, p. 301, p. 303, p. 305,
p. 307, p. 311

English translation
英訳

Christopher Stephens
belly band, p. 300, p. 302, p. 304, p. 306

English proofreading
英文校正

Christopher Stephens
p. 302, p. 304, p. 306

Figures
図版提供

©David Hockney
p. 141, p. 151, p. 201

©FLC/ADAGP, Paris & JASPAR, Tokyo, 2016 C0966
p. 119

Figures other than the above were provided by
Smiljan Radić Arquitecto.
上記以外は Smiljan Radić Arquitecto

Photographs
写真提供

Cristbal Palma
pp. 8-9, pp.22-29, pp. 32-33, pp.82-83, pp. 86-87,
pp. 89-91, pp.176-177, pp. 244-255

Gonzalo Puga
pp. 14-15, pp. 38-39, p. 43, pp. 46-51, pp. 54-57,
pp. 74-75, pp. 100-103, pp. 106-107, pp. 120-121,
pp. 130-139, pp. 152-153, pp. 158-159, pp. 166-167,
pp. 178-179, pp. 188-189, pp. 204-205, pp. 208-213,
pp. 226-233, pp. 236-237, p. 242, pp. 256-257,
pp. 278-283, pp. 288-289

Gonzalo Zúñiga
pp. 20-21, Book jacket photograph

Erieta Attali
pp. 44-45, pp. 92-93

Nicolas Saieh
pp. 84-85

Aryeh Kornfeld K.
p. 88

Iwan Baan
pp. 172-175

David Bebber
pp. 182-183

Hisao Suzuki
pp. 234-235, p. 311

Yoshio Futagawa
pp. 272-277

Smiljan Radić Arquitecto

pp. 11-13, pp. 30-31, p. 42, pp. 64-65, pp. 70-71, pp. 116-
117, pp. 124-125, pp. 146-149, pp. 156-157,
pp. 164-165, pp. 168-169, pp. 216-219, pp. 224-225,
p. 239, pp. 260-263

* The copyright holders could not be fully identified for
several items. To provide this information,
please contact our editorial department.
※数点に限り著作権が完全に判明しないものがありました。
お心当たりの方は編集部までご連絡ください。

Editorial Cooperation
編集協力

Maruzen Planet CO., LTD
丸善プラネット

Profile

Smiljan Radić

Born 1965 in Santiago, Chile. Graduated from the Catholic University of Chile in 1989 and studied at the Istituto Universitario di Architettura di Venezia. Founded Smiljan Radić Arquitecto in 1995. Named the Best Chilean Architect Under 35 by the College of Architects of Chile in 2001. Elected as an Honorary Fellow of the American Institute of Architects (AIA) in 2009. Received the Oris ACO Award for an outstanding architectural contribution in 2015. Works include the Serpentine Gallery Pavilion 2014 (London, England, 2014); House for the Poem of the Right Angle (Vilches, Chile, 2012); and the NAVE, Performing Arts Hall (Santiago, Chile, 2015). Exhibitions include the International Architecture Exhibition at the Venice Biennale (2010), TOTO GALLERY·MA 25th Anniversary Exhibition GLOBAL ENDS (2010), and the Wardrobe and the Mattress (collaboration with Marcella Correa) at the Ginza Maison Hermes (2013).

スミルハン・ラディック

1965年、チリ、サンティアゴ生まれ。1989年チリ・カトリック大学卒業後、ヴェネチア建築大学で学ぶ。1995年にSmiljan Radić Arquitectoを開設。2009年よりAIA名誉会員。2001年チリ建築家協会35歳以下の最優秀国内建築家賞受賞。2015年Oris ACO Award受賞。主な作品に「サーペンタイン・ギャラリー・パヴィリオン2014」（イギリス、ロンドン／2014年）、「直角の詩に捧ぐ家」（チリ、ビルチェス／2012年）、「NAVE——パフォーミング・アーツ・ホール」（チリ、サンティアゴ／2015年）など。展覧会に、ヴェネチア・ビエンナーレ国際建築展（2010年）、TOTOギャラリー・間25周年記念展「GLOBAL ENDS」（2010年）、銀座メゾンエルメス「クローゼットとマットレス」展（マルセラ・コレアと協働）（2013年）などがある。

スミルハン・ラディック　寓話集

2016年7月7日　初版第1刷発行

著者：スミルハン・ラディック

発行者：加藤 徹
発行所：TOTO出版（TOTO株式会社）
　　　　〒107-0062 東京都港区南青山1-24-3
　　　　TOTO乃木坂ビル2F
　　　　［営業］TEL: 03-3402-7138 FAX: 03-3402-7187
　　　　［編集］TEL: 03-3497-1010
　　　　　　　URL: http://www.toto.co.jp/publishing/
デザイン：色部義昭、本間洋史（株式会社日本デザインセンター 色部デザイン研究室）
印刷・製本：株式会社 サンニチ印刷

落丁本・乱丁本はお取り替えいたします。
本書の全部又は一部に対するコピー・スキャン・デジタル化等の無断複製行為は、
著作権法上での例外を除き禁じます。本書を代行業者等の第三者に依頼してスキャンや
デジタル化することは、たとえ個人や家庭内での利用であっても著作権上認められておりません。
定価はカバーに表示してあります。

© 2016　Smiljan Radić

Printed in Japan
ISBN978-4-88706-360-0